A TRILOGY OF PLAY

- ## THE IMPOSSIBLE PLAYGROUND
  by
  Eva Noren-Bjorn
  (Volume 1: WHY)

- ## THE ENVIRONMENT OF PLAY
  by
  John Mason
  (Volume 2: WHERE)

- ## THE NUTS AND BOLTS OF PLAYGROUND CONSTRUCTION
  by
  Paul Hogan
  (Volume 3: HOW)

THE IMPOSSIBLE PLAYGROUND

A Trilogy of Play
Volume 1: Why?

Eva Norén-Björn

Leisure Press
P.O. Box 3
West Point, N.Y. 10996

CONTENTS

Foreword

Swedish Council For Children's Play

The Council for Children's Play, established by the Swedish government in March 1971 and administered by the National Board of Health and Welfare, is concerned with play materials and environmental planning for children's play. Its main responsibilities are to advocate the importance of play in human development and to work toward assuring that good opportunities for developmental play are provided both in housing areas and public places.

In its efforts to carry out these responsibilities, the Play Council offers advice and information, arranges exhibits, and participates in conferences and discussions. In addition to these on-going activities, the Play Council has, on its own initiative, undertaken an extensive and systematic survey of how existing playgrounds and play equipment function, how children and grown-ups use play areas, and what it is that stimulates or inhibits play. Of particular interest has been the question of whether the fixed equipment found at playgrounds is really used by children and how this equipment can be improved. It seemed important to conduct such a study in order to balance all the recent attention given to safety standards and to emphasize that it is not enough to be concerned about safety when designing and selecting play equipment. In the eagerness to make play equipment safer - and as a result perhaps duller - it must not be forgotten that such equipment, to have any value, must be **used**. It makes no sense to produce play equipment which is safe and durable, but which no child is interested in using.

A Functional Evaluation Of Play Equipment

As a result of the initiative taken by the Play Council, a study of children's play activity at 27 playgrounds in Sweden was conducted for eight weeks in the autumn of 1974. Because earlier studies (Björklid-Chu,

Pia, 1974) have shown that fixed play equipment is used most in the autumn and spring, and study was resumed in the spring of 1975, at which time 19 playgrounds were visited. Four full-time psychologists accustomed to working with children and trained in the methods developed for this study were assigned the task of observing children at play, "keeping watch" over the play equipment - sometimes empty, sometimes full of active youngsters -and making a count every half hour of how many people were present in different parts of the playground. Most of the observing was done by Ulla Bengtsson, Bitte Fagerström, Märit Norenlind, and myself.

The autumn of 1974 was cold and wet in Sweden. There were recurrent storms and days of incessant rain, so that it became obvious to us that children have a need not only for lively, absorbing outdoor activity but also for some kind of warm, dry indoor space nearby.

As our study progressed we profitted very much from discussing our observations with others, particularly with Uno Dahlén and Elsa Hårdemark, who were at the time engaged in a study of children's play in neighborhoods made up of small houses. We gradually understood more and more about what it is that is especially worth noticing at a playground. We came to realize that how children play reveals a great deal about what a housing area is like, where the residents draw the line between public and private, and what contacts with the adult world are available to the children. We also became increasingly aware of children's efforts and desires to create, to fantasize, to make something from nothing, to take part, and to find something meaningful to do. And, finally, we became more and more convinced of the relevance of the environment as a whole. The general atmosphere of the area, the height of the buildings, the proximity to places of work, the distance between home and playground, the availability of loose materials and "junk", the presence or absence of involved grown-ups - all these things influence how a playground and its equipment are used. In making notes about "our" playgrounds, therefore, each of us sought to describe not only the play equipment but also the environment as a whole and its impact on children's play.

The purpose of this book is to share with others the observations we made and the conclusions we drew. In addition, it is my hope that the reader will be inspired to think about what he enjoyed doing as a child, and to begin asking questions about how much fun it really is to play in today's playgrounds where everything is ready and waiting for play - perhaps all too much so.

Surely there was much that was missing from the play environment of earlier times, but nevertheless that environment was never so lacking in variety, or in opportunities for children themselves to take the initiative, as in the average playground of today. Necessity always has been the mother of invention.

Eva Norén-Björn
Council for Children's Play
Stockholm, Sweden

1
Us Kids

"There was an old lilac hedge that ran along the road to the mill - grandpa said it was 70 meters long. The hedge had been there ever since mamma was little. It had been trimmed and trimmed, so that now the branches were thick and gnarled and there were sort of small openings and rooms here and there, just right for us kids to live in.

Linnéa was the oldest and toughest, so she had the biggest and best room. It was really nice there, for Linnéa was an only child and had an aunt in America. On the packed dirt floor was a real little rug with a nice gay pattern, almost as nice as the cloth on the table in grandpa's room. And then Linnéa had two **real** doll cups with **saucers** and an honest-to-goodness coffeepot and a small, small chair to sit on. And on the side facing the street just at eye-level there was a big peep-hole and Linnéa had hung up two little wrinkled bits of white lace with a board between, so it was just like a window. There was no limit to how splendid it was and all us kids competed with each other to get invited there.

The best thing about the hedge was that it was so thick we could be there even when it rained. Though of course we got a little wet.

I was the youngest, so I had the room that was smallest and furthest away. But there was a compost heap quite close by and wild rhubarb grew there and nothing could be better. You could chew and suck on it when you were thirsty, or cut it up in little pieces and eat it.

I began to set up house in the hedge when I was five. It took up all my time. What should I use to cook my food in? What should I eat on?

Washing the dishes was easy. Behind the mill was a lake and it became my dishpan. There was never anyone who said we couldn't go to the lake...

The first day when I was looking for things for my house I found half of a plate in the rubbish heap. It was sort of whitish-yellow with a border of blue flowers. Oh, it was beautiful! No one else had seen it because it was so dirty that only a little bit of white showed. I washed it in the lake until it shone and then took it to the hedge, where Linnéa and Ebba, Gerd and Märta, Martin and Axel, all admired my find.

Later on I noticed that grandpa's jar of shoe polish was nearly empty. Yes, I could have it all right, said grandpa. And Aunt Elsa had a cup without a handle, and in the store-house there was an old worn-out rug and I got to have a little bit of it. Uncle Ivan sawed off a couple of pieces of wood and they fit exactly in between the branches of the hedge so I had some shelves for my things.

Then Ebba and I took a trip to the blast-furnace. There were shiny, sky-blue bits of slag here, there and everywhere among the nettles. Some were flat, they were good for plates. Those that were rough and bumpy were for decoration. The nettles were awful, but we went ahead anyway and filled our pinafores full with slag bits. But afterwards our hands stung and burned, so grandpa had to rub them with potato flour. It didn't help much -but I didn't want to tell grandpa that when he had tried to help.

The next day we went to the garden. It was up on a hill, above the land belonging to the mill. There were radishes, carrots, beets, chives, parsley and spinach growing there. Grandpa even had flowers growing on his land, crown imperials and wolf's-bane, and a big elder bush. Grandpa used to dry out the flowers and then when I caught a cold I had to drink elder-tea and it tasted really awful. Along two sides of our garden ran a tall hedge that was never trimmed. The other two sides bordered on the canal and the lake . . .''

Once there had been a fine big house in the garden, but it had burned down and now there were only old moss-covered apple trees and wild gooseberry bushes and in the spring purple crocus and later white narcissus which smelled very good and in the summer Digitalis and Spiraea. The other kids called Digitalis foxglove, but Uncle Arvid taught me the name in Latin since he was a gardener.

Down near the lake we had to crawl around on our hands and knees. That's where the house stood. Then we began to poke around and look for things. I found a grimy spoon and a rusty coffee-grinder. It lay hidden in the tall grass which grew everywhere. Not a single kid went away empty-handed. Even Gerd, who was a little ''behind'', found a cracked butter-tub. And then there were green apples that we stuffed ourselves with, though they were so sour that we made faces when we swallowed them. No one saw us. And when we crawled back through the hedge, our hands and pockets were filled with treasures.

The next day Linnéa said that since I had found a coffeepot, of course we had to have a party.

From **Us Kids** by Lillie Björnstrand

2
Play and Society

That children play is and always has been obvious. But until rather recently, very little thought was given to when, where or how they played. Playing was a natural part of life. Opportunities abounded. Children had easy access to the places where adults worked, to animals and to nature. Unfortunately, however, much of this has now changed. Children today often live in a special environment, quite cut off from the working world of adults and often from nature as well. They must be compensated for this loss by being offered a play environment rich in opportunities and experiences. It is a weighty responsibility to have to plan for everything which children of an earlier time, despite frequent poverty, had close at hand: nature, work places, hidden corners, sheds and scrap-heaps.

We should not, of course, overestimate the good old days. In Sweden's present welfare society most of the poverty that was once so oppressive has been removed. But despite this there is a new kind of poverty in children's lives today - a poverty that comes from a lack of things happening, an absence of demands on them, and a want of an ideological approach to child-rearing.

Despite our goal of having children develop into competent, independent, cooperative members of society, we have in fact cut them off from community life. The most obvious deficiency in this respect is that children's contacts with grown-ups are too limited. Young women dominate their daytime world. They seldom see men, they seldom see older people, and only in rare cases do they see an adult working outside the home. Those few grown-ups whom children do see at work usually have no time to stop and answer children's questions or let them help out.

To many planners and builders, the remedy for the deficiencies in the child's environment seems to be play equipment. Unfortunately it is often the case that play equipment is introduced as an emergency measure after the planning process has already impoverished the environment. The long distances to places of work, the concentration of young families in new housing areas, and the destruction of the land's natural contours and plant growth have already ruined many of the chances to create a positive environment for children to grow up in.

It is impossible to discuss the problem of the child's world without taking into account society as a whole. A number of factors in our modern social structure make it very difficult for both children and adults to function as harmonious, integrated beings. Rita Liljeström (1976) has summarized in a striking way the reasons why people no longer feel they can understand and influence our social and cultural community:

- differentiation of activities that were once coordinated
- increased conflicts between time and interests in various spheres of life.
- incompatible rules and values in different sectors of society
- lack of a comprehensive view, overall values, and common social goals
- rapid turnover of people, places and things, high degree of mobility, instability due to constant change
- homogeneous residential areas with lack of social contacts among the residents
- segregation by age and loss of contact between people in different stages of life
- disappearance of jobs which children and young people could take responsibility for
- anonymity of large organizations and units
- increased demand for efficiency and accomplishment, increased fear of not keeping up, of failing and of being rejected
- commercial exploitation of sex, increased erotic expectations, lack of certainty about which norms are valid
- cultural stifling of free self-expression and denial of important psychological and social needs
- abundance of information, news, fiction, entertainment, and insistent advertising
- increased emotional dependence on the nuclear family (privacy, intimacy) at the same time that marriage has become less stable
- professional-client forms of psychological treatment + support
- increase in the number of experts and specialists who take over more and more aspects of people's lives, accelerated rate at which knowledge expands, creating a "culture of silence" where people do not dare to speak of their own experiences

Turning from this broad view of society to a consideration of the child's more immediate world, we realize that this world consists of a number of aspects, both social and physical: family, school, friends, books, TV, movies, leisure activities, trips, house, garden, woods, beach. All this and much more comprises the world of the child. In this book we are concerned primarily with one particular piece of this total picture, namely play areas. Play areas with their equipment are only part of a much larger whole, but nevertheless an important part since many children play outdoors much of their waking time. Just how important playgrounds and other outdoor

In interviews of children from "high-rise" and "low-rise" housing areas Eva-Lis Bjurman, ethnologist, has found striking differences in childhood circumstances, involving schooling and free time as well as future opportunities, between these two groups. A closer look at these differences suggests that it is more a matter of social class (passed on from generation to generation) than housing itself which is decisive. A study of children living in small houses (Dahlén, 1977) shows that privileges do not drop into one's lap just because one lives nearer the ground.

Child in newly-built high-rise area (father drives a taxi, mother works in a factory): "Now I'm going home to eat. I make some sandwiches myself. I'm alone. I'm always alone in the afternoons. When I am sick, I stay home alone. We have only asphalt and sandboxes in our yard. There is almost nowhere we can play. We're not allowed to be in the back and we're not allowed to ride bikes on the sidewalk. The mothers in the other yards just scream at us if we go there to swing. In our yard we're not allowed by the carpet-beating rack or by the cars. We ride our bikes in the garage. There are men there who are always chasing us away. When it rains, we're not allowed to be in the cellar or in the stairwell. I'm not allowed to have friends over when Mom and Dad aren't there. So I stay indoors alone. I draw and paint pictures. On Sundays I take care of my younger brothers and sisters. Mom and Dad want to be left alone."

Child in a "nice" single-family area (father a doctor, mother a housewife)

"It's so nice to live in your own house because then you have your own lawn. There are so many people living in big buildings.

We play a lot on the lawn. We usually kick around a ball or shoot arrows, my friend and me. It's a little far to go to the soccer field. Sometimes we go there. No, we're never chased away by bigger kids (surprised). If it rains we stay inside. Then we bounce on the sofa in the hall. Or fix up a place to do somersaults with pillows and soft cushions. Or perhaps play with cars a little. We're allowed to be everywhere except in Dad's study and in the bedroom."

areas are to a child depends on what other sources of stimulation and interaction he has.

In recent years there has been considerable discussion in Sweden about the disparities that still exist between children with different economic, social and family backgrounds. Those children growing up in older single-family neighborhoods with grandparents near by, their free time filled with activities, and the future more or less laid out for them have very different opportunities for developing their personalities and abilities than children living in large, newly-built housing developments, with grandparents far away, few choices about how they spend their free time, and little contact with adults at work. Certainly the playground serves entirely different roles for these two groups of children. For the more privileged child a static, uninspiring play area may be a needed respite from the over-stimulating and demanding environment he is often faced with. But for the child whose parents have few choices, little free time, few friends and limited chances for vacations and travel, the playground can be nearly the whole world. It is above all for the sake of such children as these that we must strive to improve the play environment by providing good play equipment and, more importantly, by increasing the opportunities for contact with involved, stimulating adults. What role does play equipment serve in the child's world? Surely it is asking too much of play equipment that it be able to compensate completely for the failure to treat the environment with care when planning residential areas. Play equipment is often added at the last moment as a sort of after-thought, to give the illusion that the planners have indeed taken into account the needs of children. But when one sees how play equipment is misused and set up in long uniform rows, with no connection whatever to the surroundings, it is hard to avoid viewing it as a kind of monument to how little planners and others know about children. The usual response to such criticism is that other, admittedly better, solutions are unfortunately not feasible. Indoor areas, play leaders, loose materials and involvement of the residents in decision making are desirable but not possible. Fixed, rigid equipment is a compromise, or perhaps a symbol of having given up.

Whom are we to blame for all this? The planners blame it on stingy local officials and builders, on "users" who do not care and on unimaginative manufacturers. Local officials, in their turn, blame it on lack of money and on other priorities, while the manufacturers in their turn blame the planners for setting up the equipment in such a way that it cannot function as it should. There are even those who say that the whole situation is the fault of unconcerned, inhibited mothers! Up to now, however, it has been the manufacturers who have been attacked the hardest. They are blamed, and often rightly so, for producing dull, bad equipment.

What determines which types of play equipment are sold? Naturally in a free market economy what is produced is that which is most easily sold. Most companies have their own designers who come up with ideas which are then discussed back and forth within the company. Sometimes the Play Council is consulted, but the companies are under no obligation to follow

Bidrag till
bättre
boendemiljö

Bostadsstyrelsen 1975

its recommendations. The most common method of product development has in fact been to plagiarize the catalogues of other manufacturers. One important change that has taken place in recent years is a shift from steel to wooden construction.

In 1976 the Play Council, the National Board of Consumers, and the manufacturers together formulated some general guidelines regarding play equipment. The manufacturers agreed to stop selling dangerous equipment, and to provide full information on proper assembly and maintenance and also, eventually, on how the equipment is in fact used by children. This last is to be the result of an objective functional evaluation of how children actually use the equipment in question, what type of play it leads to, what age children use it, and whether children using it play alone or with others. Up to now, the information provided by the manufacturers has been based on how the equipment is **intended** to be used, which - as our study has clearly revealed - is often an entirely different matter from the **actual** function which a piece of equipment has.

In discussing who the "culprits" are in the playground controversy, we should not forget that, while all the involved parties share the guilt, economic policies and a planning process that allows for too little participation on the part of those affected are also to blame. Residents themselves must be given the right to decide how money set aside for maintenance and improvement is to be spent. They must be able to plant their own flowers, and to decide for themselves where parking lots and playgrounds are to be located. There are many who have neither the time nor interest to be concerned, but there are surely others with the energy and will to work toward improving the outdoor environment for themselves and their children. Not until these resources are tapped will it be possible to create a housing environment that is a positive asset to people of all ages.

Since 1973 government grants of up to 50% have been available for the improvement of residential areas. A large share of the 30 million Skr spent annually under this program goes to help purchase play equipment. Making play equipment is profitable, and many hopeful new manufacturers have gone into the business. Someone benefits from sprucing up dreary environments with play equipment, but it surely is not the children.

3
Functional Evaluation

How can we know which types of play equipment are good and which are not so good? Safety and durability are important factors, and much attention has rightly been paid to them. But we at the Play Council have felt a great need to focus attention on other aspects of play equipment as well and it is therefore that the study on which this book is based was begun. We were particularly interested in finding out what is stimulating and developing for children. We wanted, in other words, to assess the developmental aspects of play equipment. To make such an assessment requires an understanding of developmental psychology and a method for finding out if particular types of play equipment lead to growth and development. It is meaningless, as has already been said, to make equipment as safe as possible if it is not going to be used in any case. Play equipment, to be used, must provide a certain degree of excitement. For children, playing is often a matter of overcoming a fear of heights or of falling, of training skills and of practicing how to control one's body. If play equipment is too safe, if it is too low, if all risks have been eliminated, then it is boring and children do not use it. It is easy, therefore, for safety requirements and functional requirements to come into conflict.

In the effort to make playgrounds safer, people are apt to forget too easily that children look for excitement wherever they can find it, as these two childhood recollections make clear:

"... We used to climb up on the roof of a tall building and play soccer there. To get there we had to climb up a drainpipe the last bit of the way. Sometimes it was a little loose, but that didn't stop us. It makes me shiver to think of it now. That we dared ..." (A man reared in a suburb of Stockholm)

"... We used to crawl into the elevator shaft and sit down **on top of** the elevator. The strange thing was that there were rugs there. Someone had discovered the place before us!" (A woman reared in a small town)

If playgrounds are too dull, then children will go play on roofs or in elevator shafts, in parking lots or shopping centers. According to a study made by L.H. Gustafsson in 1975, only about 5% of childhood accidents occur at playgrounds and about 3% while using play equipment. The danger to children is considerably greater at home and in the rest of the residential area, above all in traffic. Besides working to make play equipment and play surfaces safer, we must realize that it is just as important to children's welfare to make playgrounds an attractive alternative to playing in other more dangerous places.

When discussing the safety standards for play equipment, it is essential to take into consideration how the equipment functions. It makes a big difference if a child can understand the dangers involved in doing something, or if the dangers are hidden from him. It is not possible to foresee that a piece of equipment may suddenly fall apart or that an arm can get caught or a foot broken because of poor design or construction. Moreover, many apparently obvious risks may not be obvious at all, especially to young children with limited experience and judgment. A swing in motion or a child rushing past on a sled or bike can be dangerous to the small child, who is much too egocentric to realize that he himself constitutes an object that can get in the way of someone else.

The kind of risks that we need **more** of in playgrounds are those which, from the child's viewpoint, are calculable. Objects which involve movement at high speeds (aerial ropeways, steep slides, go-carts, etc.). High climbing frames or roofs where only the most skillful can reach the top, long ropes attached to tall trees, and high suspension-bridges offer the chance for calculated risk taking. Only those children who know that they dare and can will use such equipment. There is a hierarchy of skill and courage among playmates which older children are often fully aware of, and each knows his own capacity and limitations. One factor, however, which must be taken into account is that a child may be forced by peer pressure or everyone else ganging up on him to do something that is beyond his skills. For this reason hazardous equipment is recommended for supervised playgrounds only.

The purpose of the Play Council's study of the functional value of play equipment has been to appraise the value of fixed play equipment, loose play materials and the play surfaces themselves. Materials brought from home or discovered by the children on their own, as well as materials provided at the playground, have been included. The evaluation is **not** based on such considerations as durability or correct installation but rather on what is pleasurable, stimulating and developing for children. The theories of developmental psychology together with our own extensive observations form the basis for our judgments.

As one result of this study, we wanted to be in a position to give advice and recommendations as to **which properties of play equipment** increase its functional value. We have not been interested in rating the products of particular manufacturers, but in reaching fundamental, general conclusions which can later provide a basis for a possible functional description of specific products on the market. Our ultimate goal is to stimulate the production of good equipment and discourage the manufacture and purchase of dull or dangerous equipment.

Sub-goals of this study have been to determine which components characterize "good" play equipment and developing activities, and to work out a method for making functional evaluation of play equipment.

To be able to judge what equipment is good and how the environment should be designed to promote children's development, it is necessary to have a theory about how children develop and what promotes and inhibits this development. We have taken as our starting-point that view of human development which regards the child as an active, inquisitive individual who, through play, exploratory behavior and social interaction, acquires knowledge about his physical and social environment and about himself as well. Developmental psychological theories, and the play theory of Jean Piaget in particular, lie at the very heart of this study. We need therefore to take a closer look at what these theories can tell us about children and their play.

4
Play—What Is It?

The many definitions of play

To be able to plan for play something must be known about what play is. There is no definitive answer to the question "What is play?" but rather an overwhelming variety of attempts at definition, based on descriptions of different types of play, classifications and sub-classifications of play, and theories of play. What is obvious from all of these, as well as from the attitude of children at play, is that play is important. But in what way is play important? A number of different theories have been proposed in answer to this question, several of which we shall discuss here.

In the popular literature on children it is common to classify play and games according to content. Creative play, fantasy play, construction play, active play, passive play, imitative play, playing alone, playing with others, water play, sand play, playing ball, playing house, playing doctor, winter play, summer play, indoor play, outdoor play ... the number of possibilities are endless. Categories are devised to describe what children do, what materials they use, whether they are alone or in groups, if they are indoors or out, what season it is. Such classification systems are not based on any theory about child development but are more of a hodge-podge listing of what children do and experience. Automatically attaching the word **play** to **whatever children do** does not bring us any closer to understanding the role of play in development of the child. We must look elsewhere for help.

In carrying out our study we have relied primarily on two theories of child development, the cognitive theory (which is mainly concerned with intellectual development), as found in the work of Jean Piaget, and the psychodynamic theory (which is mainly concerned with emotional development), as found in the work of Lill Peller. Both theories include descriptions and explanations of the role of play in development. When we were observing the behavior of children on playgrounds, we found that the cognitive theory, and specifically Piaget's theory of play, proved to be the most fruitful. To apply the psychodynamic theory to observations of children requires that one be able to interpret the child's innermost feelings, and in a study such as this one involving so many different sites and different children, this was clearly impossible. On the other hand, the psychodynamic theory proved very useful when it came to **interpreting** why, for example, children enjoy doing different things at different ages. For our purpose it has worked very well, therefore, to combine these two theories.

Play and development
according to Jean Piaget

Jean Piaget is a Swiss psychologist who has been interested since the 1930's in the origin and structure of human thought. As one way of approaching this problem, he began to study children, both his own and others'. Piaget found that play and imitation have a decisive importance in thought formation and that they are in fact tools which the child uses to make the world his own. In the course of his work he developed a theory of play, which offered a new view of the intimate relation of play to the total development of the child.

According to Piaget's theory of human development, the individual has two strategies at his disposal for dealing with his surroundings, **assimilation** and **accomodation**. The human being is continually striving to find an equillibrium between assimilating the external environment to his own needs and accomodating himself to the external environment. For the small child, the environment is a constant challenge since he keeps coming across new objects, new emotional reactions from others, and much else which he must both absorb and adjust to. An example of the extreme form of assimilation is the kind of play where the child takes material from real life and adapts it to fit his particular view of things, distorting it in keeping with his own desires and previous experience. The extreme form of accomodation is imitation, where the child's behavior is governed entirely by an external model. Piaget believes that the child uses play and imitation to help him incorporate reality into his own conceptual framework as well as to adopt to the demands of this reality.

The following situation illustrates this process at work. A child picks up a flower, hangs it against the table and sucks on it. When the child meets the resistance either because of the nature of the object or because of the reaction of someone or something in his surroundings, he must hunt for other patterns or behavior from his repertoire of motor activity and combine these in a new way in order to be able to deal with the "new" object. An adult shows him how to hold the flower carefully by the stem and smell it. The child imitates this behavior and puts the flower up to his nose. The

Climbing a tree constantly provides new challenges for coordinating and adapting physical movements. With every step upward the body must find a new balance, the strength of the branches must be tested, new difficulties must be overcome. The structure of the bark, the form, color and smell of the leaves, and the swaying of the tree in the wind together provide a total, vital, rich experience.

Can a man-made climbing apparatus replace all this?

child, in other words, has adapted his actions to the object with the help of the model which the adult provides, and an equillibrium is reached. In order to reinforce this new way of holding the flower, the child repeats the action in the form of play. In this way he solidly enlarges his repertoire of behavior patterns.

In Piaget's opinion, play is one of the ways the child has of relating to his surroundings. Another way, as we have seen, is imitation, where the child repeats a sequence of actions without in fact having any understanding of what he is doing or any chance of basing his behavior on previous experience. There are, of course, many intermediate forms between play and imitation, where the child uses his talent for imitation in his play, as in make-believe and mimicry games.

Another way for the child to relate to the world is exemplified by actions in which assimilation and accommodation are in equillibrium, so that the child carries out appropriate actions which neither distort reality (as in pretending a block is a boat) nor are fully controlled by how someone else handles an analogous situation. In this case the child has the chance to use his earlier experience according to what the external world requires. This is what happens when, having acquired certain skills, he uses them to carry out some form of goal-oriented work.

Having mentioned work, it may be worthwhile to pause a moment before continuing our discussion of Piaget's play theory to take a look at the distinctions between play and work. In an article on playgrounds (Institute of Psychology, University of Uppsala), Anderson, Höök etc. state that play is just as meaningful for children as work is for adults. They differ in these ways:

- Work is necessary. We work so we can get the resources we need to live.
- Play is voluntary. One does what one wants, when one wants, where one wants.
- Work is a response to external pressures from family and society
- Play is a response to internal needs and desires. Play is necessary for the individual himself, in order to maintain a healthy balance in his life.
- The main goal of work is a product. The value of work is measured in terms of quantity and quality.
- Play as a process is valuable and an end in itself. The play itself, not some product of it, affords satisfaction.
- Work is carried out in accordance with external set rules and regulations.
- Play is based on rules which the one playing decides for himself, i.e. internal rules which can easily be changed.
- Work is carried on in the real world. Real things are produced and sold.
- Play is not confined to reality. Objects in the surroundings can represent whatever the child himself wishes.
- Play is an expression of human freedom.

Piaget's play theory

Piaget's play theory is based on the notion that the various forms of play come about naturally as a direct consequence of the level of development reached by the child, provided of course that the environment promotes development.

Play in young children

At that period when the child is learning to crawl and walk and is trying out all his senses, his play consists of repeating movements and sensory impressions for the sheer joy of experiencing the functioning of his own body. This type of play Piaget calls practice play. What is involved in such play (also called functional play) is voluntary practice, **not** enforced training, of sensori-motor skills. Examples of this type of play include going up a hill and rolling down, balancing on a railing, turning somersaults, splashing in the water, tossing blocks out of a chest, letting sand run between one's fingers, and throwing stones. Play always involves doing something both pleasant and voluntary. However, play can easily pass over to problem-solving and experimentation. The child may want to try pouring water into a hose instead of just splashing, or to balance on a bike rack instead of on the edge of the sand-pit. Or he may try to build a tower out of blocks, get a seesaw to balance, or sort out stones after some principle. Such activities require adaptation to reality, and they promote development. The child can then expand his play repertoire by using his new skills. Old forms of play become uninteresting as he grows older and new forms take their place. It is always those activities which contain elements of both the familiar and the

Practice play goes on for many years even though it is the dominant form of play for only the very youngest children.

unfamiliar that attract the child most and are the most developing. Piaget expresses a firm belief in the child's own ability to hit on just that activity which, given his current situation, leads to further development, as long as he is free to choose his activities and his playmates and gets a response from, identifies with and is stimulated by active adults around him.

It is important to be clear about what Piaget means by an environment that promotes development. He is **not** speaking of some sort of training laboratory where children can raise their I.Q. or speed up their development, but rather of an environment offering a rich variety of experiences at whatever phase of development the child is passing through. The supply of concrete experiences of materials. human reactions, and feelings collected during childhood serves throughout life as a firm foundation for thoughts, intuitions and emotions.

In the bushes or under a rock there is a lot to discover, whether one is big or little. Imagine that a wood-louse rolls into a ball if you poke it! (Orrhamnaren, Arsta)

Play changes character

When the 1 1/2 - 2-year-old begins to develop the ability to think and to imagine things that are not present in time or space, the character of his play changes. At this time objects and people in his world cease to function solely as things he can look at, touch, taste, smell or use to satisfy his need for movement. They become bearers of properties that the child ascribes to them. The child can now **pretend** to do things! This type of play is termed symbolic play by Piaget. The child begins to play in a way that makes use of his talent for symbolic representation. A stone is not only fun to bang and throw, it can also be transformed by the imagination into a car whizzing along the edge of the sand-pit. At first the child is content with a very superficial resemblance between object and reality; it is often enough if one or

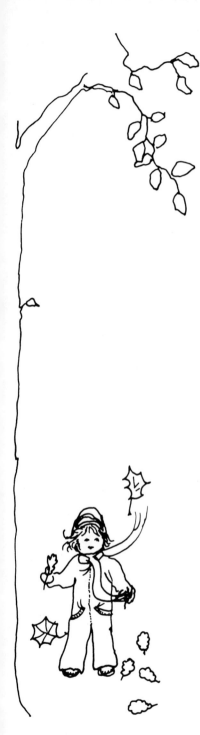

"Mommy, if I was big I could take down all the leaves so it couldn't blow anymore!"

two properties of the actual object and its imagined form correspond. A doll need only consist of a cardboard tube with two eyes and some hair to be quite satisfactory. This is related to the level of concept formation which the child has reached. He may at this point call everything with four legs "bow-wow", everything that gives light "lamp", and anyone who takes care of him "mommy." In other words, the child attaches importance to just a few properties of the objects and people in his world. Only gradually does he become aware of further complexities.

As the child's ability to imagine and to understand increases, symbolic play takes on a different form. It begins to include more and more of those experiences which the child encounters in his life. The very earliest games consist of the child's performing actions in play which normally belong to his daily routine, such as pretending to sleep or eat. In the next phase, he transfers everyday situations to a teddy bear or doll. Gradually the child is able to use his talent for imitation to mimic someone doing something that he himself has never engaged in directly, like driving a car or sweeping the floor. Symbolic play can involve the child giving form to something or someone using his own body; he can represent a church, a policeman, or a gate that keeps people out. Or the child can pretend that an object is something else: a block becomes a man, a popsicle stick a comb, a mossy stone a troll. In the higher forms of symbolic play, these two aspects are combined and the child stages simple scenes where he himself "is" someone else and where the objects used are regarded symbolically. The child can, for example, pretend to undress a playmate and give him a bath. He feels the bath water, rubs him with soap, rinses him off and dries him. This kind of play, according to Piaget, provides an opportunity for several types of emotional responses to experience. The child can do something forbidden, as when a little girl warned by her mother not to pick up her baby sister pretends to rock the infant in her arms. Or the child can re-live some difficult or unpleasant situation, pretending, for example, that his teddy bear is going to the dentist, or that he himself is a dead bird which he saw and was frightened by. The child can also, through play, indulge in fantasies concerning the consequences of not obeying an order or following advice. One way to do this is to tell a story about a pretend playmate who did not do what his mother said, and what happened to him then.

Play gets richer

Piaget divides symbolic play into **three stages**. All that has been described so far concerning symbolic play belongs to stage 1. This stage lasts until the child is about four years' old.

At the age of four the child has a certain ability to explain his opinions and actions and to form concepts. He is still dependent, however, on having concrete materials as a support for his thoughts, he is still strongly influenced by what he sees and experiences at the moment, and he still finds it difficult to take into consideration several different aspects of a situation at once. The child's way of thinking is egocentric, which is why it is common

for children at this age to attribute life and feelings to an inert object and to believe that natural phenomena are caused or controlled by human beings. An example of what is typical for this age group is a comment by three-year-old Henrik one very windy day: "Mommy, if I was big I could take down all the leaves so it couldn't blow any more!" Due to the child's increased capacity for thought and his broadened experience of the physical and social environment, symbolic play gradually becomes more diversified and organized. Children strive more and more to give an accurate picture of reality and they begin to divide up roles more realistically. When playing mother-father-child, it is no longer good enough to have two mothers in the family. Instead, the children reach agreement among themselves about who is going to be mommy, daddy, big sister, guest, etc. Realism at this stage is still limited to what the child "knows" of life, and distortions to suit his egocentric desires and his limited experience are still common. Trying out different roles through play helps the child to grow out of his egocentric way of thinking and provides a broad foundation for his developing ideas. Stage 2 of symbolic play lasts, according to Piaget, until the age of seven, at which time the first games with rules begin to make their appearance. Rule games often arise out of practice play. The child begins to be interested in what he must do so that various materials will act in a certain way. How should he adjust to variations in weight, length and form if he wants to hit a target or get a ball to bounce just the right amount? At this point, the possibility of rule games arises.

At the beginning of this phase, temporary rules are worked out when the situation demands. For example, some children playing together may agree that they are only allowed to step on the lines and cracks in the sidewalk. This kind of rule play fills a very important function, since it is a stepping-stone leading to the ability to understand the more complicated fixed rules that come up in games and sports later on.

A reflection of reality

Before we go into greater detail about rule play, however, we need to consider the final phase of symbolic play, that which is characteristic of children in the early school years (ages 7 - 9). At this stage the child distorts reality less and less in his play. Instead, in both acting out and constructional play he tries to copy reality as closely as possible. A typical example of this was observed by me in my neighbor's yard one August afternoon. Several children between the ages of four and twelve were pushing baby carriages around over the hilly ground. It was hard work, and they complained loudly the whole time about how difficult it is to have to push around a baby. They offered to help each other, expressed their thanks, and discussed all their problems. "Wouldn't you just know there's no escalator!" "You can sure tell who it is that decides things around here!" A twelve-year-old girl set the tone and the others all chimed in. That this occured in a backyard and not at a playground is unfortunately all too typical. For play to reach this level of development at the kind of playgrounds we have today is very unusual.

A girl throws a stone in the water. She listens to the plop and watches the rings forming. Another girl comes up and tries to "hit" a target in the water. The girls begin to keep score of how many times they get a hit and to discuss what "counts".

Surely each of us remembers that this is just the way we used to play when we were little. Another example may help prod your memory. Two boys are playing together on a farm in the summer of 1974. The boys are brothers, six and eight years old. Their parents take care of the farming, and their grandparents have retired to a smaller house on the farm but continue to take an active interest in what is going on. The boys have built a house for themselves, about 1.5 meters square. It has a sloping roof and is painted red. They have covered the roof with corrugated sheet-metal and attached a metal drain pipe, which they have lengthened with several boards fitted with edges. The water runs into a barrel. The house has a chimney and several windows, one of glass with a white lace curtain. Inside the house they have hung pictures on the walls, and on the home-made stove is a coffeepot. In a cupboard, which consists of a box standing on end with shelves, all sorts of containers are lined up in neat rows. The door has a bolt and a real padlock. The key hangs on a nail near by. Close to this house is a smaller house which has sunk down a little into the ground and has brick walls. It is a food cellar, they explain. Next to it is a plastic barrel buried in the dirt. The eight-year old shows us how it works. He fills the barrel with water, then gets out an old pump and fits it into a hole in the lid. When he puts on the lid and starts pumping, water squirts out of the spout. The boys are even considering adding water pipes! They already have a drain from an old sink which they have installed next to the stove inside the house. We ask about a cover we see lying on the ground; "Is this the well?" "Not exactly", they reply and giggle. They show us a pipe that goes down into the ground right next to it. "This is to pee in" they say, and grin. The area around the house is partly enclosed and the boys have set up a gate which they always go through, even though it would be easier to go around it. In the yard they have some hay and a cart. Later we learn they each have their own scythe, small ones that are just right for them.

"That one, he's not so dumb, he's not" says the boys' grandfather referring to the older boy. "He has ideas, that boy. Why, just think what they can make out of nothing!"

This example shows clearly the socializing function of play. The boys' parents and grandparents are farmers and this is naturally reflected in their play. Socialization among city children must of course take other forms.

We can also see from this example that planning and realistic construction are the most important elements in the final phase of symbolic play. At this stage the child integrates all his knowledge and experience of people and events. The symbol, which previously was a distortion of reality designed to suit the ego, has now developed into an aid to the child in his adaptation to reality.

"Just think what they can make out of nothing . . ." At the playgrounds we have today the word "nothing" is all too literally true.

Rule games

The most important change that occurs in the child's way of thinking at about the age of seven or eight, besides being better able to consider many aspects of a situation at once, is the increased capacity to identify with another's feelings and assume another's role. Just as symbolic play makes use of the ability to fantasize, so rule play uses the ability to make and follow social agreements. It is first when the child grows out of his egocentric way of thinking and realizes that **each** person is an ego center and that everyone stands in relationship to everyone else (so-called socio-centered thinking) that following common rules becomes possible. Examples of rule games are tag, follow-the-leader, hide-and-seek, hopscotch, jump rope, soccer, hockey, ping-pong and so on. For all these games there are established rules which are passed on as a sort of play-culture from one generation of children to the next. Piaget has remarked that names and rules often take on local color but that at first children feel very strongly that a game must be played exactly as they have learned it. It is as if a higher power has decided the rules once and for all. Paradoxically enough, at the stage when children are most rigid in their notion of following the "right" rules, they are not yet able, intellectually, to realize when they and others have broken the rules. When children gradually come to understand that every group can make its own rules if everyone agrees, then they also are better able to perceive rule violations. At this stage the child is fully ripe for rule games. Endless discussions often arise over the rules, and they can sometimes end in quarrels, causing the game to break up. These conflicts are very important, however, if the child is to develop the ability to understand all aspects of the rules and their application, and they also offer a chance to practice social skills. The will to continue with a game is usually strong enough that discussion leads to constructive solutions.

A hockey club can "be" many things. To fence and shoot is a way for children to work through the scenes of war and violence they can hardly avoid seeing on TV. "Playing off" anxiety is pleasurable. But no adult needs to sanction war as a proper way to solve conflicts by giving children war toys!

Lill Peller's play theory

Piaget deals with play above all as a part of the development of thought, although in no way denying its physical and emotional importance. However, since Piaget does not give central prominence to the emotions, it is both interesting and worthwhile to complement his theory with the psychoanalytic approach to the role of play as proposed by Lill Peller (1954). Peller sees play as a means for the child to absorb experience bit by bit. The playful repetition of an event enables him to handle painful situations and to turn from passivity to activity. One way for the child to do this is to switch roles in his play; instead of being the anxious on-looker or the suffering party as in real life, he takes the initiative or turns aggressor. Another time the child may change the outcome of a situation, providing a "happy ending." The very fact that the child can re-enact an unpleasant experience in play constitutes a switch from passivity to activity and makes the experience more pleasurable.

All play involves wish fulfillment, pleasure, elation, a feeling of euphoria and well-being. Still, play is not only a direct manifestation of the pleasure principle. It is also an attempt to compensate for anxieties and deficiencies, to obtain pleasure with the minimum risk of danger, punishment, or irreversible consequences. Play is a step toward sublimation; through it, ordinary life finds its expression in higher forms of creativity. One often finds creative or artistic activity described as a "regression in the service of the ego", a voluntary return to an earlier stage of development so the individual can draw power and inspiration. The same might be said about play. Play is of great importance in enabling us to feel like integrated beings, with emotions and thoughts in harmony.

Peller has drawn up a schematic summary of the "topics" that appear in play at various ages. She presents this in terms of four Groups, each with its characteristic topic. A topic is defined as something the child wishes to deal with and come to understand through his play. This schematic table (Table 4-1) indicates which topics the child handles at various stages of development, according to psychoanalytic theory, what deficiencies he experiences and how he finds compensation through play. With the appearance of chronologically later play groups, the earlier ones do not disappear but persist, perhaps in a modified form. This is especially true for Group I activities, in which the child works out his relationship to his own body. Fantasies of increased physical strength and skill are incorporated in all play. We see from the table how effectively the two theories—that of Piaget and that of Peller—can be combined. At no point do they contradict each other. One can say that Piaget contributes insights into the structure of play while Peller gives us a picture of the emotional content of play.

The topic of play during the early years (Group I) has to do with the relationship of the child to his own body. The child imagines grandeur and perfect ease and his play is attended by feelings of elation and pride. The

Table 4-1 The stages of child development according to Peller and Piaget

Peller			Piaget	
Topic	Deficiency	Compensation	Structure of play	Type of play
Group I, 0 - 2 years Relationship to one's own body	"My body is no good. I am helpless."	"My body is a perfect instrument for my wishes."	The child explores the possibilities of his own body purely for the pleasure of how it functions.	Practice play
Group II, 2 - 4 years Relationship to the mother or the adult closest to the child.	"I am little and helpless. You can do what you want with me."	"I can do to you what my mother does to me."	The child transfers simple everyday actions to other people or objects	Symbolic play Stage 1
Group III, 4 - 7 years Relationship to the adult world.	"I am little. I am excluded from grown-up pleasures."	"I am big. I can do what grown-ups do.	The child reproduces an entire sequence of events from the adult world. Children divide up roles among themselves and strive for a certain degree of realism even if their own wishes still are a strong incentive for distorting reality.	Symbolic play Stage 2
Group IV, 7 - 12 years Relationship to one's peers.	"I must look authority in the eye, defy threatening authority completely alone."	"I am not alone. We are a group and we are united. We follow the rules to the letter."	The child uses his capacity for social agreements and for following common rules.	Rule play
	"I cannot be little again and start all over."	"I can begin again as often as I like. I can live not just one but many lives."	The child depicts scenes from reality. The planning of play and the construction of realistic accessories are more important than the playing itself.	Symbolic play Stage 3

child tries to lengthen and broaden his own body and he fantasizes about his great strength. A shovel is better for digging than his hand. A wooden block makes a better hammer than his fist. A ball skips and rolls without danger of a painful fall or bruised knee. Play with sand, water and mud can replace playing with feces, which is socially unacceptable. Implements used in play are experienced more as improved versions of body parts than as tools, and they have a strong emotional value for the young child. When we grow up and our muscular power and suppleness more nearly correspond to our desires, such play decreases. But since our bodies remain imperfect, fantasies of greater skill and potency persist throughout our lives.

The theme of play in Group II concerns the child's relation to the person who most often takes care of him, traditionally the mother. Such play derives from fantasies about the mother as the inexhaustible source of caring and comfort, but also from fears which are due to the child's total dependence on her. Through play the child can make his doll or teddy bear the recipient of maternal care or possible rejection. In hide-and-seek games, he can defy his mother and escape in a playful way from her domination and protection. In addition, through play the child can take on an active role and can behave toward others as his all powerful mother behaves toward him. The first animal play usually appears at this period. The child can transfer his image of the mother to a stuffed animal without deleting any essential traits. Hence animals may arouse in him feelings of great tenderness, fear, admiration or hilarity. Furthermore, through his play the child incorporates both "the wicked mother" and "the good mother." Later on he will use his aggressive instincts for positive purposes, and he will get energy from the associations surrounding the image of the good mother when things go badly. To gain a more subtle view of people as individuals with both good and bad sides, the child needs at this stage in his play to have symbols for the good and the bad, the familiar and the unknown, the safe and the terrifying. We recognize this pattern from fairy tales, where each figure exhibits a single pure trait: Bashful, Happy, etc. and the wicked stepmother.

The topic for play from the age of about four to seven is the child's relationship to the adult world. Play during this period is much more varied. Using many different settings, rules and disguises, the child pretends to possess privileges which in real life are reserved for adults. At this age, the child's play is at its most imaginative and the games are often intense interpretations of reality. Children try to play together even though they still have trouble managing to understand one another. Accessories associated with adult life are important for role creation, and play often deals with adult life in such a way that the child assumes adult privileges and enjoys them without any guilt feelings. The child experiences a heady feeling of happiness, even triumph, in his play. Every player is a hero who can command fate. Group III play activities often continue in the form of fantasies up into the early school years. The child, feeling that his parents do not correspond to the dream of an ideal family, may imagine that they are not his real parents or that he would be much better off without any parents.

Figures like Tarzan and Robinson Crusoe are favorites. The hero's survival is due entirely to his own valiant efforts, his courage and his inventiveness.

Being together with others, maintaining loyalty, observing rules and keeping track of what others are doing are characteristic features of children's play from the early school years to the early teenage years (Group IV). Play changes character about the age of seven or so, improvised and emotionally laden play being exchanged for well-organized play where the formal elements dominate. The child looks beyond his immediate family. He is attracted by friendship with peers but also by the idea of attaching himself to new father and mother figures among older friends and teachers. Games and sports emerge out of dreams of belonging to a brotherhood where everyone mutually and jealously guards his special prerogatives or follows a chosen leader. The topic for play at this stage is the first liberation from parents. Strict rules are the backbone of games and the child regards them, for the duration of the game, as absolute. This makes the child independent of external superego figures, such as parents and other authorities. In games it is often more important to observe the rules than to win. Competition is important, to be sure, but if all those taking part hold strictly to the rules, then the winner and loser can shake hands afterwards and return to their former state of equality. Games are also distinguished from imaginative play in the matter of how the child experiences time. In earlier play the child can start over as many times as he wants. There is always a new chance. The clock is turned back and the player resumes his initial position as many times as it suits him.

A theory is a theory and not "the truth"

The theory of developmental psychology can provide us with a model of how development proceeds and how play fits into this process. What the theory cannot give us, however, is a definition of what sort of development is desirable. We must decide ourselves on the direction of this development, in accordance with our ideology and value judgments. That children give expression in play to family situations and are pre-occupied with liberation from the family is no accident but the result of the culture of our times. A child who already at a young age has the chance to form close attachments to a number of people and to grow up in an environment where solidarity and comradeship between generations is stressed will have another content in his play and will perhaps not experience liberation from the family and the step out into life as such a conflict-inducing situation. Chinese preschool children act out plays about heroes in poetry, dance and song at the same age that Swedish children are playing mother-father-child. The capacity for empathy, imagination and expression is present in preschool children the world over. What differs is the content that children are provided for their play, and this depends on the particular culture in which they are growing up.

We work to earn money

We work to serve people

-from Rita Liljeström's "Our Children—Others' Youngsters"

Through play the child absorbs the values of his society.

5
The Role of Play in the Social Development of the Child

Play and interruptions

We have seen that practice through play leads to genuine learning in the case of concepts rooted in feeling as well as in thought and action. With this in mind, we can now ask what true role of play is in the social development of the child, that is in his "maturing" in the social sense. A Finnish researcher, R. Helanko, in an article about the relation between play and socialization (1958), points out that play is not the same for children as for adults. What adults regard as play in a child's conduct is often not play at all. An activity such as painting a boat can start out as play and then shift to work without any observable change in behavior taking place. It is the attitude that changes; the action becomes purposeful. Play occurs less often as the child grows older because the number of disturbing systems increases. If a child who is playfully painting a boat feels in the mood to do something else, all he has to do is put down his brush and walk away. A grown-up, on the other hand, feeling the same desire to do something else, will normally make an effort to finish what he is doing first. At that point he is no longer playing, he is working. It is only on rare occasions that an adult can enjoy totally undisturbed play.

Play and socialization develop side by side, according to Helanko, during the early years. They are connected with each other in various ways, but they are not strictly comparable. Play is a particular attitude, while socialization is a lengthy process of development. Those factors that interrupt play, like needing to go in and eat, tie a shoe, or decide who may join in a game, promote the socialization of the child, just as play itself is.

The factors which disturb play are thus important to the child's development. The very young child's first play system soon becomes uninteresting to him. What was once fun no longer feels like fun as he gets older, even though he may remember how much fun it once was. Earlier systems are replaced by more advanced ones. Systems that at one point in a child's life disturb play may later change character completely. Thus a piano lesson once experienced as a "must" taking him away from play is later regarded by the child as play! If it were possible to create a first play system without disturbing factors, one which the child was totally satisfied with—which no normal child would be—then learning would be very limited and development would cease.

Since the systems that interfere with play usually promote socialization, there seems to be an apparent incompatability between play and socialization. But if the interfering systems were removed, both play and socialization would suffer. Play seems to act as a restraining factor in development and is in that sense somewhat conservative. It provides the child with some refreshing breathing-space from the arduous demands of the process of socialization. Play and non-play are like two counteracting hormones which must be kept in equilbrium.

Stop planning for play!

When one considers play as a part of the child's total development, it becomes obvious that it is all wrong to design special places for play. What is needed by the child is a wealth of opportunities for experience and self-expression in his total environment. Then the child himself can decide if he wishes to make use of these opportunities. For the child to thrive and develop, he needs to be offered a variety of experiences, including chances to participate, take responsibility, be useful and work side by side with grown-ups on meaningful tasks. Gathering branches to make a fire, raking leaves and carrying them to the compost heap, or cleaning up are just a few of the activities that children can be included in doing. With patience and an instinct for his abilities and attitudes, and sometimes with the help of play, an adult can familiarize a child with grown-up jobs and how they are done. It is important that the child's increasing powers and skills be put to use and that he be given the chance to be helpful to others.

What children need in addition to a wealth of experiences is a variety of opportunities to express themselves. In order to deal with experiences, to digest them and to understand the roles, conflicts, and problems that are involved, the child must have access to materials through which he can communicate. Such materials can be anything from dress-up clothes to pen and paper, building blocks and plants. Play is a way for children to get a grip on reality. Children need a wide range of opportunities both to experience reality and to give expression to this experience.

Play and reality

respect for
the child's need
for play
for the liberation
of joy
the joy of living
the joy of trying
the joy of knowing more
respect for
the child's need
for reality
as the raw material for play
as demand and confidence
that one can manage
as a spur to further growth

6
Children Need
to Move About

"Not to let children move about is a sure way to tire them out." Stina Sandels.

Since so much play equipment is intended to give children the opportunity to develop their motor skills, it is important to take a closer look at the child's need to move about and how this is expressed at different ages.

The ability to move, to stand, to walk, to handle objects is central to man's development. By his way of moving, the child expresses his feelings of joy, disappointment, enthusiasm or anger. With the help of movement he can also change his feelings; he can cheer himself up or give vent to a disagreeable feeling and then shake it off. Movement can also be a way of acting out something, of enabling the child to become a swaying tree or a closing gate.

Through his own actions the child acquires experience of the causal connections that govern the physical world. Movement thus becomes a basis for the formation of logical concepts. In the early years of life sensorimotor development dominates completely. The small child experiences an enormous variety of contacts with the people and objects in his surrounding. It is these experiences, with all their qualities of smell, color, structure, weight, texture, etc., together with the many and varied explorations of his own body and its possibilities, that determine the course of his future development. Later, when the child gradually begins to increase his conceptual powers and to engage in logical thought and abstraction, the multitude of early experiences forms the basis for and gives nourishment to this intellectual activity. If the child is prevented from moving, from experimenting or from forming close emotional ties when young, then his later development and creativity will be seriously impaired.

Development of motor skills - from the top down, from the inside out

The child's ability to coordinate his movements, control his own body and move with precision and skill develops slowly the whole time he is growing up. Muscle growth even during the teenage years is so great that the average child increases the percentage of muscle weight in relation to total body weight from 33% at the age of 15 to 44% at 16. At birth the muscles comprise 23% of body weight, and at the age of eight 27% (Bentsen 1971). We see then that children's muscles grow considerably throughout the school years. This is not because the child acquires more muscle fiber but because he is using and training those muscles he has had from birth.

There are certain fundamental facts concerning the physical development of the human body that those who plan children's environments should be familiar with.

Control of the muscles progresses from the head to the foot, and gross motor skills are mastered before the finer ones. A small child moves his entire arm instead of only his hand. Young children therefore need a lot of room and large playthings suited to the type of movements they are able to make.

Lack of coordination and precision in the movements of young children is due to the fact that the nerve paths which conduct impulses from the brain to various groups of muscles are not "isolated." The young child's reactions therefore involve the entire body. A one-year-old who has just learned to walk often cannot stop without sitting down. A child just under two who throws a ball with one hand makes the same motion with the other hand as well. It is first at the age of three that children are able to coordinate their muscles so that they can run round a corner without making a wide arc. It is said that this "embedding" of the nerve paths is hastened through **practice** - that is to say, through play.

Different muscle groups are developed at different stages of the child's growth. We have two types of muscles which work together and enable us to move and stand upright, namely bending and stretching muscles. In the small child it is the bending muscles that dominate, as can be seen from the way an infant keeps his arms and legs bent in toward his body. As the stretching muscles gradually develop, the child is enabled first to stand up, then to walk. At certain periods it is the stretching muscles that dominate. This is expecially apparent at the ages of six and eleven; children at these ages have a special liking for stretching out, for reclining in chairs, for climbing and for lying full length on the floor.

The smaller the child, the heavier the hammer must be . . .

Children get tired faster than adults

Because children's muscles contain a greater percentage of water than those of adults, they tire more quickly and must change position more often. When children are given the chance to choose their own work position, they **change** position often, shifting among various ways of sitting, standing and lying. A variety of surfaces and the freedom to function in accordance with their own nature and to alternate between being at rest and being active are essential if children are to make the best use of the physical powers they have. It is very important to take this into account when planning environments to be used by children.

7
Plus and Minus in the Margin

What conditions in the child's environment influence his development?

In order to be able to evaluate the child's environment as well as his play equipment and play materials, it is necessary to take a stand on the issue of what "good" play is.

The term "good" play is not very satisfactory since it is easily misunderstood. Some adults interpret "good" play to be that kind of play which is neat and tidy and in which nothing ever gets broken! Another problem is that **all play** should probably be regarded as "good." Let us then call that type of play which we have in mind **developing activity.** By "developing" is meant development in the "good" sense, not that a child is pushed to learn to read at the age of three, but that the child has a rich range of experiences at whatever his current stage of development.

By studying children both in real life and as they are described in literature and research, we have come up with a catalogue of certain feelings, behavior patterns, experiences and modes of self-expression which are characteristic of children and what they do and which must be regarded as essential to development. These have to do with play as well as work, dealing with reality as well as influencing it. Both sensory and emotional experiences are considered, as well as different forms of expression. These aspects of child behavior and the child's world are presented here as a list of positive and negative features. Such a list, we feel, makes it easier to understand what is in the best interests of the child in the long run.

Time
+ Play lasts a long time and is intensive. It evolves and develops the whole time.
+ Play is interrupted but then resumed again.
- Play stops due to a shortage of space and materials.
- Play is spoiled by competition and aggression.

Level of development

+ The child makes use of materials at his own level of development. A chess set, for example, can be used in different ways by children of different ages. Two-year-olds move the pieces around and pretend to play, four-year-olds may play according to some principle they themselves have thought up, eight-year-olds learn to play correctly in accordance with simple rules, etc. That which is at the same time familiar and also a little new is most inviting.

− Materials are restricted by their nature to play which is is mostly on a level lower than that which the child has reached. This happens, for example, when materials for make-believe, creating and building are lacking and all the available equipment is designed for vigorous motor activity or when there is neither the equipment nor space for rule games.

− The child fails often, gets hurt, and is continually prevented by others from trying these things out.

− The child is not tempted to try things out. Everything is familiar and easy, the child feels bored. Frustration and boredom can result in part from the tendency to build special play areas for young children but can also be due to the fact that those responsible for planning children's environments are unaware that children have different abilities and needs at different stages of development. It is difficult, but despite that it is necessary to plan an environment suitable for all ages.

+ The activities appeal to children and grown-ups regardless of the age and all can have fun together.

− Grown-ups cannot find anything to do. Their need for contact is in conflict with their job of keeping an eye on their children. They are passive.

Social life

+ The child can decide for himself if he wants to play with others or alone.

− The child is forced into being part of a group. Or the child is alone, without any playmates.

+ Playing together is a positive experience. Cooperation, consideration for the rights of others and a feeling of comradeship are encouraged. The child is protected against "the law of the jungle" and conflicts are resolved constructively.

− Being together with others leads to conflicts which are often resolved by the strongest winning.

+ Life offers many experiences of being together with people of different ages and backgrounds. Closeness to other children of various ages gives the child a sense of the continuity of his own growth and development. The younger children can look ahead to what they will become. The older children can be childish when they need to, or they can serve as authority-figures and feel useful looking after and helping others.

− The child grows up with only young women around.

− The child plays only with children of the same age. Games are not passed on from older to younger children. Conflicts between different age groups are typical.

– Children see isolated adults who do not belong naturally to any social network.

Possibility of influencing the environment

+ Children are allowed to destroy in order to understand. They can clean fish, take apart a motor, look inside a seed, tear down a hut to build a new one. The children use scientific methods to explore their world.
– The environment is so "finished" that every change is regarded as destructive.
+ Children and adults have a real influence on their immediate surroundings. This applies to management and care as well as decisions about important changes.
– Children and adults feel powerless to influence anything. Decisions are handed down from above. In the worst case, those who take care of things are viewed as enemies whom it is fun to sabotage.

Variety

+ The surroundings give children the feeling that the world is full of things worth exploring.
– The surroundings are sterile, there are few materials, there is too little space.
+ The children have access to a wide variety of sensory experiences. Different smells, rough and soft surfaces, warm and cold objects, beautiful and harsh sounds, sweet and bitter tastes all heighten the awareness of the world around us, especially when we are children.
– The surroundings are all man-made, carefully arranged. Plants are off limits to children, and children are to be seen but not heard, to look but not touch.

Freedom of movement

+ The child has a chance to explore his own body and to experience the pleasure in movement. He gets to feel his stomach sink, his head spin, his whole body tingle. He has a chance to jump into something nice and soft, to swing and feel light-headed, to float and experience weightlessness, to turn the world upside down.
– Children are kept from moving about, changing positions when they feel like it, and doing such things as balancing, jumping, hanging, turning, riding, swinging floating.

Language and thought grounded in action

+ The child verbalizes his experiences and in this way transforms concrete actions into ideas, which later leads to the ability to imagine actions without actually performing them. The child's mother tongue serves as the framework for his thoughts, and he has continuous contact with an adult who speaks that language.

– The child receives no verbal response to his actions. The adults do not give names to things and they do not interpret with words what the child does. Language is mostly encountered in "two-dimensional" forms, i.e. in books and on TV, without any connection to the child's own actions. Children of immigrants are offered a verbal foundation in a language not native to them.

Processing, assimilation and interpretation

+ Play serves as an aid to the child in dealing with his experiences and over-coming problems and conflicts. Play can be a way to compensate for being little, work through a family conflict, handle the fear of being left alone, express anxiety about growing up. Play can help the child to deal with his sexual identity or provide an outlet for the wish to do something forbidden.

+ Play materials can be altered or with the help of imagination be used in accordance with the child's own ideas and desire to express himself.

– Play is not permitted to develop freely in keeping with the child's own needs. The child is kept from dressing up, splashing in the mud, hitting a doll.

– The child gets only "ready-made" play materials which can not be changed without being destroyed and which can not be used in a variety of ways depending on what the child himself wants to do in his play.

– Play materials are regarded as something the child owns and which confer status on the owner, instead of being regarded as a means for the child to do, express or create something.

Emotional involvement

+ The **whole** child is involved. The child experiences with all his senses, reacts emotionally, uses gestures and physical movements to express himself, considers and comments openly and without inhibitions. He responds to and is stimulated by the reactions of others. He experiences things totally and fully.

– The child is bored and uninterested because of the lack of stimulation and social interaction. The child is inhibited or else overactive and destructive.

Links to reality

+ The child becomes acquainted with a vital everyday world, its cultural life and working life. He is exposed to a variety of adult roles, sees adults actively cooperating with each other. The adults have time to include the child in their work, give him a chance to help out according to his abil-ity, make use of his increasing capacity to work and take on responsibil-ity. These experiences are absorbed and dealt with in the form of play.

– Children live among other children and those who take care of children. They see only the negative effects work has on grown-ups, that they got tired and do not have time or energy for their children. They see few active adults so they lack roles to imitate and use in their play. The child's ability to assimilate reality in the form of play goes to waste.

+ Play materials relate to an actual social reality. Dolls have everyday and work clothes as well as fancy dresses and folk costumes. Vehicles and work tools are copies of real ones and make complicated technical concepts familiar to children. Play materials are real, usable objects which stimulate the child's creativity.

− Play materials reflect values which are not a part of the society in which the child is growing up. The child is presented with a false dream-world in which dolls are all ballet dancers or soldiers, reflecting stereotyped sex roles. Play materials provide an idealized picture of overconsumption, of violence and war. Man's everyday reality is denied.

Freedom of choice

+ The child chooses freely on the basis of his own needs and desires what he will do and with whom. He decides what he wants himself or together with others.

− The child is forced, directed or "motivated" by an adult to do something. A particular activity is to last for a certain period of time not decided on by the child himself, and he is put in a social situation not of his choosing, or forced to be alone. The child is steered from without, so that what he does is not in harmony with his own needs.

Dialogue and interaction

+ Child and adult together explore the real world, shoulder to shoulder. The starting-point for explorations of nature, social life, technology, language, politics are those questions which children and adults want to find answers to. Adults serve as a source of knowledge and contribute their ability to see the larger picture and their experience.

− The adult steers the child's learning process by deciding what subject the child should be interested in at a certain time either by compulsion or by creating the necessary motivation. The adult asks manipulative questions with "right" answers. The adult lets the child participate in life through the experience of others. He is the active party and expects the child to be the passive recipient of what he has to give.

Should play equipment satisfy every need?

Naturally not every item included on this list is equally important or open to observation. In our study we have concentrated on those aspects that we have felt to be most relevant, and we have moreover taken into account what is possible to learn by the method of studying the behavior of children with whom the observor is not otherwise acquainted. It is important to emphasize that play equipment can hardly be expected to satisfy all these developmental needs. It is total environment, not just the playground or even the housing area, that must offer overwhelmingly positive opportunities to the growing child for sound development.

8
Definition of Functional Value

According to the definition used in this study, functional value refers to the capacity of a play surface or piece of play equipment to stimulate children to play, work, experiment, and relate to others, or in other words to engage in developing activity that is both pleasurable and voluntary.

When this study was first begun we used the term "play value" to describe the **qualitative** aspect of the utilization of play equipment and play surfaces. But we found that **play** is an ambiguous word which means something different to each person who uses it (somewhat like the word happiness), and which moreover is encumbered with both positive and negative associations (i.e. "They do nothing but play in school"). We have chosen, therefore, to use the more neutral words "function" and "functional value."

Functional value is also a more appropriate term than play value given the theoretical foundation we have chosen. As Piaget points out, play is only **one** aspect of those processes which carry development forward. Functional value covers not only play, therefore, but also social interaction, imitation, exploratory behavior, experimentation, and learning as well.

The statement that a certain type of play equipment "has" a certain functional value is to be understood as referring the way the equipment is most often used. There are exceptions, of course, since such factors as access to loose supplementary materials, a child's earlier experiences, and above all the amount of stimulation provided by adults have a great significance for how play unfolds. Nevertheless one can say with a considerable degree of certainty that children of different ages have characteristic ways of acting which are a consequence of the level of development they have reached. Consider a ball, for example, whose primary characteristic is roundness. The functional value of a ball for children of different ages will vary with the child's ability to throw, catch, fantasize, interact with others and follow rules. By changing the secondary characteristics of the ball—its surface, color, size, weight—it can be made more or less suitable for a child at a certain stage of development: For the child about a year old who is practicing the finer movements of the hand, a little ball or a ball with a highly textured surface can have a high functional value. For the child learning to walk, a large ball or a ball which can be carried around or kicked about has a high functional value. For the school-age child a tennis ball or soccer ball can have a high functional value. In this case the functional value varies depending on the qualities of the ball combined with the child's ability to understand and follow the rules being applied.

In this example we can recognize the various stages of play which, according to Piaget, a child goes through. We can say that a ball has a high functional value in general since it is amusing for all ages and can be used in a variety of ways for different types of play. But the notion of functional value includes more than just play.

Activity adapted to the demands of reality

Another component of functional value has to do with the degree to which play equipment and play surfaces encourage exploratory behavior, problem solving, learning, or work.

Exploratory or investigative behavior occurs when a child, as a result of his own activity or change in the environment, is confronted with a situation which he has not before mastered—in other words, a problem. When the child is able to adapt his actions to the new situation and in this way recover his balance, learning has taken place. The child does not, however, learn only by seeing, hearing and feeling, that is, by incorporating sense impressions. The child influences and changes his surroundings and in this way creates problem situations himself. Just as the scientist does, so the child increases the number of natural occurrences in order to see what will happen. The child experiments, puts forward hypotheses, tries them out and observes the outcome of his own actions. By manipulating materials he improves his knowledge of the world. The older the child is and the more factors he notices, the more refined is his interpretation of the world around him.

The learning process is set in motion when a child first experiences some task as difficult and then manages to adapt to the new situation. Once learning has taken place, it is often followed by repetition in the form of play.

The new knowledge is in this way assimilated. If, however, a task proves to be too difficult so that the child either gives up or fails, then the problem leads neither to adaption nor to learning. Situations at either extreme, whether **too easy** or **too hard,** lead to boredom and frustration and not to development. That activity which offers just enough challenge and which is engaged in with pleasure and/or concentration is that which leads to development in the child.

Work, which is purposeful action with a specific goal, is another example of this type of activity. Work gives the child a chance to try out his ability, to be useful, to participate in creating something. This can involve helping to build a small hut, planting and watering flowers, carrying leaves to the compost heap, pushing a baby carriage, helping to put away loose play materials, making a fire for roasting hotdogs, shovelling snow, or feeding a pet. Everyone who has had experience with children knows how eager they are, if the conditions are right, to be useful. Play is no goal in and on itself. When children have acquired certain skills they want to put them to use and to feel that they can be part of a social context. It is not true that children play up to a certain age and then shift to work. Play and work alternate in their lives with a fine balance. As was mentioned in the chapter on play and social development, Helanko (1958) emphasizes that it is just this interaction between play and adaptive or—as he calls it—compulsory behavior that leads to development and to socialization to the child becoming a part of the adult culture around him. This adaptive behavior gives the child new knowledge, while play provides the chance to process and assimilate this knowledge in a relaxed, undemanding way. As the child gradually is able to manage more and more adult actions, he has less need of play. There is a shift instead to a need for relaxation and variety through sports, hobbies, creative activity, fantasy and day-dreams.

Social interaction

A third component of functional value has to do with whether play equipment or a play surface is conductive to positive social interaction among children and between children and grown-ups. The main principle to keep in mind when speaking of positive social interaction is that a **reciprocal** exchange is the most advantageous and that a lop-sided dominant-submissive relationship does not favor development.

An extremely important part of social interaction is the contact between child and grown-up. The adult as model, stimulator, supporter, protector, someone to confirm impressions, and a fixed point from which the child can make his voyages of discovery is of very great value for all children and essential for small children. The adult is, in other words, a **central figure** in the child's play environment, and his presence is very often a prerequisite for a play area to function well. The adult can stimulate play by providing children with those materials that are needed if play is to be able to develop. Some equipment cannot be used without adult help, as for example swings in the case of a two-year-old. For older children, the adult functions as model, as someone to play games with, as one who explains, confirms, protects, or suggests how to resolve a conflict. Even a passive adult can be an

important figure, since children who are used to relating positively to adults feel reassured by the mere presence of one. But surely an active adult who takes pleasure in being with a child, likes sledding or playing ping-pong together, or who enjoys relaxing or working with other adults is the most stimulating model for the child. Play equipment or a play area which encourages adults to be active or which favors joint activity between children and adults is thus given a high functional value.

Conflicts between children are not necessarily something negative since they can offer a chance for children to work together to solve differences that arise. On the other hand not all conflicts are conducive to development. It is how a conflict is resolved that determines the extent to which it can be regarded as positive. A stimulating environment with access to grown-ups and a full, varied assortment of materials increases the chances for healthy solutions to conflicts. It is also necessary that the parties involved be on a somewhat equal footing.

Close contact with others is the most important experience our environment can give us.

Sensory and emotional experiences

An important consideration which has already been mentioned in connection with play, work and social interaction, but which deserves to be discussed separately as well, has to do with sensory and emotional experiences.

Consider the situation of three girls, 5 - 7 years old, who are walking around on a half-frozen puddle. It is exciting when the ice cracks under their feet and the water seeps through. The whole body must be used to keep one's balance on the slippery surface. Various sensory impressions are combined with feeling of joy, tension, and fear. The social interaction heightens the fun; the children urge each other on and they try more difficult things, like walking faster and tramping harder.

This example shows how intimately entwined the cognitive, physical, and social factors are. It is important that children have a chance to use all their senses and to learn to coordinate and interpret their impressions. An environment which provides a whole range of sensory experiences therefore has a high functional value.

Emotional experiences are an important driving force in development. These can be of different types. There are physical feelings, such as the tickling in the stomach that comes from sliding fast, swinging high or jumping from high up. Other sorts of feelings are involved when a child solves a problem or manages to balance on a high beam or succeeds in hitting a lamppost with a stone. These can be called cognitive emotional experiences. Then there are those feelings which a child experiencs towards other people, and which can be called social feelings. All these kinds of emotional experiences are relevant and important in determining functional value.

Frequencey of use

Something else which obviously influences functional value is how much a piece of equipment or play surface is used. A high rate of use does not necessarily mean a high functional value, however. One must also consider how it is used, by which age groups, and what other alternatives are available.

It should now be clear that functional value is a sort of qualitative value system where many combinations are possible and where one can not state unequivocally what is "good." One can not, for example, say that playing with others is always best. Nor is experimental behavior always best. Perhaps it is not even possible to say categorically that play as a form of pleasurable repetition of a learned activity is **always** good. It is a range of choices, a wide variety of possibilities that must be the goal in shaping play environments for growing children.

- Is there somewhere I can go and be left alone if that's what I want?
- Is there the chance for interaction with others?
- Can I experiment with changing the environment?
- Can I concentrate on working with something if I want?
- Can I relax and play in a way that makes no demands and enables me to work through the impressions which the real world has provided me?
- Can I take part in a game where I voluntarily submit to rules in mutual agreement with others?
- Are all these activities enriched by emotional and sensory experiences?
- Do I have a chance to get protection and support from an adult?
- Is there an adult who can confirm my impressions of reality, who can listen, ask questions, provide new perspectives, explain ideas, and stimulate me to new kinds of activity and play?
- Do I have a chance to become familiar with real grown-up life?

If the answer to these questions is yes, then the play environment functions well.

9
Scope and Method
of the Study

When have the children been observed?

This study has involved a total of 28 play areas, 27 of which were visited in the autumn of 1975 and 19 in the spring of 1976. Each period of observation lasted eight weeks. The various playgrounds have been studied with different degrees of intensity depending on the size, number of children and types of play equipment involved. In most cases the observations were sufficiently thorough that the observer has been able to state with considerable certainty how a playground functions and could immediately note any unusual occurrence. Observations were made both morning and afternoon, during those hours when the playground was most heavily used. We cannot say anything about how the playgrounds function in the evening. In the case of older children, this means that we have observed their afternoon but not their evening games.

It is play during the week, when the children cannot go away with their families and absorb new impressions, that we have studied. In the evening and on weekends other pleasant experiences are possible - if a child is lucky enough to be born to the "right" parents.

Choice of season

The playgrounds have been studied in the autumn and spring, August 15 - October 15 and April 15 - June 15. We have not analyzed winter play but believe that fixed play equipment is of less importance then. Those types of equipment that involve very vigorous movement can function well, but

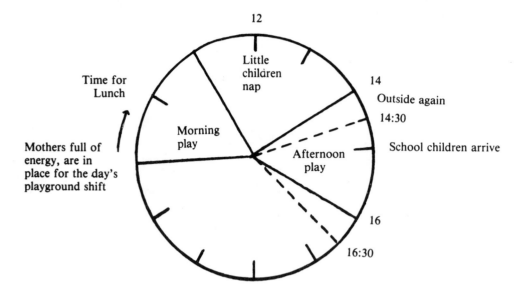

otherwise it is snow and ice that are important for winter play. In the summer the playgrounds are largely abandoned in favor of swimming and sunbathing. Wading pools, showers and lawns with water sprinklers are very popular, however. Nevertheless, we feel that it is adequate to understand how fixed play equipment functions during that part of the year when it is most patronized, that is, in the spring and autumn.

The playgrounds have been studied both morning and afternoon. The exact times have varied somewhat depending on the time when each particular playground had the most visitors

Method

Playgrounds and play equipment and the children using them were studied for a total of 640 two-hour shifts, including both morning and afternoon periods. During one of the two hours of each shift, a single child chosen at random was followed for up to 40 minutes. The observer recorded minute by minute where the child was, which type of play equipment or activity he was involved with, whether he played with others or not, and how pleasurable, concentrated or interrupted his playing seemed to be. Notes were also made on what the child said, the loose materials used, and any emotions manifested. At the end of each period of observation a note was also made on what contact grown-ups at the playground seemed to have with each other, and what contact the child under observation had with the grown-ups present. Assuming that an observer followed a particular child 30 minutes on the average during each two-hour shift, these observations

If there are no hills for winter sledding, they can be built up from excavation materials, or a temporary wooden hill can be set up! (Tessinparken)

would total 19,200 minutes for the entire study. In fact, the actual number of minutes recorded in the study is 16,157, of which 6,389 were during the autumn and the rest in the spring. The autumn figure is lower because the frequent rain meant that there were often few visitors at the playground.

Furthermore, during every two-hour shift the number of children using different parts of the playground was counted each half hour. This method unfortunately proved to be too inflexible to allow any definite conclusions to be drawn. The figures have been used primarily as an aid to the memory when preparing descriptions of the different playgrounds.

During the second hour of each two-hour shift, two pieces of equipment were observed for a half hour each. It was often difficult to record any observations, however, since most fixed equipment is used relatively little.

The playgrounds have been described in terms of how children and grown-ups use them, what it is that attracts children there, which surfaces and equipment they choose for their play, and which physical and psychological factors in the environment seem to promote or restrict play and personal contacts. To help in describing the physical environment of the playgrounds, we have used the five dimensions presented in a report entitled Children and the Physical Environment, prepared by the Swedish Commission on Children's Outdoor Environment. These dimensions are accessibility, variation, adaptability, spaciousness and privacy, all viewed from the perspective of the residents of an area. Given our special purposes, we have interpreted these dimensions in such a way that they could be used together with our systematic observations to determine how good or bad playgrounds and play equipment are.

What kind of playgrounds have been studied?

We have only studied local playgrounds (those within sight and hearing distance of home), neighborhood playgrounds (those with a somewhat larger catchment area) and supervised playparks (municipal playgrounds with trained staff); no preschool or school yards have been included. We have selected playgrounds in as many different kinds of residential areas as possible, including both inner cities and suburbs, both private homes and apartment buildings. We have studied both old and new playgrounds with only a little equipment as well as ones crowded with equipment. In order to study how successfully fixed equipment competes with loose play materials, carpentry, water play, care of animals, access to fire, and gardening we have also chosen playgrounds where all this was available. In other words, we have aimed at including as many different kinds of playgrounds as possible (Table 9-1). Furthermore, we were interested in studying the same type of equipment in at least three places in order to be able to compare how it functioned in different environments and draw some general conclusions. As a guide in the selection of sites, we obtained lists from various manufacturers of playgrounds to which equipment had been delivered.

No school or preschool yards

We have not studied play equipment in school and preschool yards, but a few general observations can be made here. To some extent preschool yards function like local playgrounds. One can assume that the fixed equipment is quickly "used up." To some extent this can be counteracted by stimulation from adults who play with the children, tell stories, and arrange visits to places like fire stations and harbors and then encourage the children to give expression to and re-create their experiences in play. If less emphasis were put on having "finished" play areas, it would be possible for children, staff and parents working together to make changes and revitalize the children's interest. It is not necessary to view equipment only as a monument to bad planning. It can also be a starting-point for creating something new of one's own!

Table 9-1
Schematic summary of the variations among the playgrounds, studied in terms of type of residential area, size of the catchment area, presence of staff and indoor facilities, and type of surface and equipment.

	Carpentry corner	Fire	Gardening	Water	Animals	Natural terrain	Artifical surface	Concrete deck	Play park	Neighborhood playground	Local playground	Shelter: Roof	Indoor facility	Unsupervised	Supervised	Little fixed equipment	Much fixed equipment
New suburb, apartments																	
Orminge	X						X		X						X	X	
Fisksatra	X	X	X	X			X		X						X	X	X
Upplands-Väsby	X				X	X	X	X	X						X	X	X
Nyby	X						X		X						X	X	X
Husby		X		X		X	X		X						X	X	
Spångaby		X	X			X		X			X				X	X	X
Hallonbergen	X(X)					X		X							X	X	
Tingvalla						X					X		X		X		X
Vårdaren						X				X			X				
Ekilla					X			X					X	X			
Bellman						X				X			X				
Brandbergen						X		X		X			X				
Older suburb, apartments																	
Eriksberg	X				X	X		X					X	X			
Stigsberg					X					X			X	X			
Orrhammaren						X			X				X	X			
Inner city																	
Humelgården			(X)		X	X		X					X	X			
Tessinparken			(X)		X	X		X					X	X			
Draken (newly-built)			X			X		X					X	X	(X)³		
Haren			(X)			X		X				(X)²	X	X			
Fältöversten (newly built)						X		X					X		X		X
Stadsparken			(X)		X	X		X					X	X			
Geijers					X	X		X	X				X				
Stamgårdsparken			(X)			X				X		X	X			X	
Båten						X				X			X				
Barrsätra						X				X			X				
Area with detached private homes																	
Näsbypark						X		X					X	X			
Viby (newly built)						X				X			X	X			
Sandvik (newly built)						X				X			X	X			

(X) = drinking fountain
(X)² = situated off to the side
(X)³ = much equipment added after the observation period ended

The case of schoolyards is somewhat different. In school, children unfortunately have little chance to move about in keeping with their own needs of the moment but instead must conform to a set schedule. This happens despite the fact that we know full well children and adults have different requirements when it comes to moving about because their bodies are different. In schools, therefore, there is almost always a pent-up need among children to move. Putting climbing equipment in the school yard is a poor substitute for letting children alternate between activity and rest, change position, climb, and stretch in the classroom. It is worth repeating here what Stina Sandels has said: "Not to let children move about is a good way to tire them out."

How many types of play equipment can we give an opinion on?

This study includes the greater part, though not all, of the play equipment to be found on the market in Sweden. A total of 208 individual pieces of fixed play equipment have been observed, not counting swings and sand-pits, which are present at almost all playgrounds. These have involved some 50 different types of fixed play equipment. Of these, 2/3 have been observed at three or more different play areas, and about 5/6 at no fewer than two places. Eight types have been observed at only one place. Of these eight, five are similar to other equipment observed so that conclusions can be drawn about them. There are, however, four types of equipment that it is hard for us to give an opinion on: and boats. The last-named, boats, have been observed at three places, with differing results depending on their design.

10
Main Conclusion

Sand is nice and one of the few materials found at playgrounds which children can influence and change after their own ideas.

The main conclusion of our study is that most of the playgrounds found in Sweden today are designed so that they cannot be altered either by children or by adults. They cater mostly to play of a "repetitive" nature and very rarely do they stimulate experimental and exploratory activities. The more developing sorts of play, those that give the child a chance to process experiences or grasp and assimilate new knowledge, seldom occur. This is partly due to the fact that children very often live in a world devoid of interesting occurrences and meaningful contacts with the many aspects of adult life. This means, in turn, that they have too little raw material, in the way of experiences, and models, to use in their play. Moreover, unsupervised playgrounds in particular lack creative materials that can be used and reused by children in many different ways according to their own desires for expression. Nor do playgrounds as a rule satisfy the need adults have for contact, stimulation and meaningful activity.

Fixed play equipment is often designed so that it is too difficult for younger children and too boring for older children, who quickly master it. Most fixed equipment is used for a very limited percentage of the time children spend at a playground. Swings, sand-pits, and slides fastened to a slope constitute an exception, as well as large combination climbing frames and loose materials like bikes, carts, excavators and large chests of building blocks. Low equipment for climbing and balancing, backboards and fixed representational equipment like houses and store-fronts at places where loose materials are lacking are not used at all.

It is the ground surfaces together with movable equipment and loose materials that are used most. Much of the fixed equipment only stands empty, taking up valuable play space.

11
How Unsupervised Playgrounds Are Used

Those playgrounds which we are now going to discuss are referred to by the name of the neighborhood or housing area where they are situated. In this chapter the following unsupervised playgrounds will be considered: "Brandbergen" in Handen, Haninge township; "Fältöversten" in the Östermalm district of Stockholm; "Tingvalla" in Märsta, Sigtuna township; "Bellman" in Uppsala; "Sandvik" in Viksjö, Järfallä township; and "Stamgårdsparken in Sundbyberg.

As can be seen from Table 1, we have calculated what percentage of time the observed children have spent using fixed play equipment as opposed to the various playground surfaces. The fixed equipment is divided into two groups, namely swings and sand-pits, and all other fixed equipment. The table shows that children normally spent 50 - 60% of their time playing on the various surfaces, and that the total for ground surfaces plus swings and sand amounted to 70 - 85% of the time the children were at the playground. In no case were there only a **few** kinds of equipment available. At Brandbergen, for example, there are 12 different pieces of equipment, not counting swings and sand-pits.

Swings can be enjoyed by children of all ages. For the youngest, swinging means feeling snug and a pleasant tickling sensation in the stomach. Older children play together on the swing, talk, sing, and push each other.

Table I. Percentage of time, on the average, that the children observed spent on fixed equipment and on ground surfaces at **unsupervised** playgrounds.

Name of the playground	On surfaces	On swings and in sand	On other fixed equipment	Total
Faltoversten	59	18	23	100
Brandbergen	52	33	15	100
Tingvalla	55	14	31	100
Bellman	49	28	23	100
Stamgardsparken	50	33	17	100

Note: At Sandvik playground the open surfaces where the children play were beyond our field of observation so comparative figures can not be given.

It is interesting to know in more detail just what kinds of surfaces and equipment are used most. Appendix I presents this information, giving the percentage of time in use for each type of fixed play equipment and surface at the different playgrounds. Equipment and surfaces are listed in order, beginning with what is most used. To make the situation even clearer, the list is divided into two groups: those surfaces and equipment which, taken together, are used 75 - 80% of the time, and those used 20 - 35 % of the time. We can see from this appendix that such surfaces as asphalt, sand, gravel and grass, as well as sand-pits, always appear high up on the list. Among the types of equipment most used are swings, slides, and in a few cases small or large combination equipment that are standing idle most of the time.

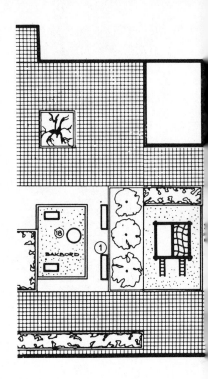

Fältöversten

Fältöversten
Residential area
The area known as Fältöversten is a newly-built housing complex located in the Östermalm district of the city of Stockholm. The buildings and play areas are built on a concrete deck above the level of the shopping and service center and the underground.

The buildings in the complex are long and high. The size of the open areas in relation to the buildings is such that they lie mostly in the shade. The area is entirely free of traffic, with a pedestrian path leading across to Tessin park, where there are large grassy areas, a wading pool and a supervised play park. All the playgrounds at Fältöversten itself have about the same equipment, with the exception of the yard connected to the day-care center, which has two slides. In the center of the area is a wading pool.

The playground is mostly in the shade.

Design of the playground
As the site-plan shows, the playground is a very long and narrow rectangle. It is entirely flat and paved with concrete slabs. The equipment is arranged in square sand-pits, all with baking sand. What greenery there is is planted in cement containers. Some of the bushes are periwinkle. There are no bushes with edible berries. The equipment includes a large climbing frame with rope ladders and netting, and two different types of smaller combination playhouses, one of a type called Hags lill-poly-play, and two so-called peak-houses. Swings, sand-pits and a little house with no roof are also present, along with a ping-pong table and a backboard for playing ball. There are benches by the sand-pits and ping-pong table.

Shady and windy
The playground is always windy. It lies mostly in the shade. Only in the morning before 10 o'clock is there sun. In the summer when the sun reaches

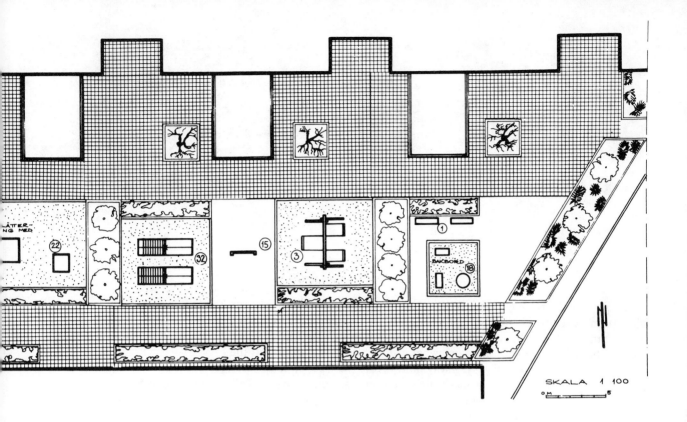

over the roof-tops it is sunnier, but the problem then, according to the parents we have talked to, is that it can be terribly hot. There is no protection from wind or intense sun nor the kind of pleasant sun-shade variation that large trees provide.

A passageway

The playground is very handy, just outside the entry doors, and children and grown-ups can reach it without crossing any street. This is clearly the playground's greatest advantage. Nor does it contain any dangerous equipment. On the contrary, there is a lack of equipment that can provide a little excitement for children above the toddler age. In other ways also it is a very uninspiring place. Grown-ups experience it as boring, and one seldom sees children under three there since those parents who must accompany their children obviously prefer to go elsewhere. The playground gives an overall impression of monotony. The equipment is arranged stiffly at more or less regular intervals. The plants which separate each area are raised somewhat above ground level so that the space feels broken up rather than unified.

The playground is not set off in any way from all that goes on around it. It can seem both deserted and crowded at the same time, probably because of the relationship between the play area (long and narrow) and the sur-

rounding buildings (high and fairly close together). One side of the playground ends with "nothing"; there is a fence facing the street below, which can give the feeling of being unsafe. When the trees get leaves in the spring, the overall impression is somewhat cozier. Because the area has the character of a long, narrow passageway, and because there is so much running in and out of the doors, games which are begun are often interrupted. There is no secluded corner where a small group of children can develop their play undisturbed by others.

Grown-ups hurry past.

The playground serves as a passageway for children too.

One sees few grown-ups outside except for those who pass by on their way in and out of the house. Nor is any particular contact among them noticeable, even if some of them recognize each other. On a beautiful day it has happened that several adults have sat in the sun and talked a while, but otherwise most people seem anonymous. Moreover, the adults have very little contact with the children playing outside except to call to them to come in or go to the grocery store. The children seem quite abandoned as long as they are outdoors, but it is quite possible that they are "looked after" by their parents from the windows and balconies. The number of children present varies considerably from one moment to another. Children run in and out, or temporarily leave to go play elsewhere. Since everyone who wants to leave the area must pass through the playground, many take a quick turn on the play equipment as they go past.

The children play together in small groups, mostly with others of the same age. Often two or three children play together for some time while an outer, continually shifting ring of children forms around them. Some children join in for a little while or stop just to look before continuing on. Larger groups of children can often be seen together, but for the most part they do not play anything special. The mood among the children can be fairly tough, and there are certain children (boys) whom the others are afraid of. The following situation was observed one Friday morning toward the end of April.

A large wall is needed for playing ball. The backboard is much too low.

When equipment is grouped together like these peak-houses it has many more uses.

"Cold and grey. Very few children out. Dreary atmosphere. A group of boys, age 7 -10, come and go, obviously bored and without anything to do. Try at one point to provoke the observer. At another point, disturb a boy of about six playing in the sand and chase him around so that he has to go and hide behind the laundry house to get away."

Conflicts arise rather often. Most of them are resolved, it seems, by each one going his own way.

How the play equipment was used.

None of the equipment was used particularly frequently, considering the large number of children passing by. The sand-pits were used sporadically by children 3 - 10, and now and then by even younger children. To play bake-a-cake and such games, the sand around the fixed equipment was used just as much as that in the sand-pits.

The little round house without a roof was used occasionally for sitting in or climbing on, but never for imaginative play.

The backboard was never used for playing ball, but sometimes it was used for climbing. The children preferred to throw ball against the door of a supply room. In another yard, however, there is a larger backboard and high ventilation shafts which the children use for playing ball.

The two peak-houses were used by children 3 - 10. Preschool children used the houses to live in, huddle in, or have as a foundation for playing bake-a-cake. They also played dolls and mommy-daddy-child there. The older preschool children were able to get up onto the roof and slide down. Older children played different kinds of tag, often using both houses at once and jumping between them.

The small combination climbing house with slide was used by small children for climbing and sliding, although not particularly often. School children, taking a detour past it, would quickly climb up and slide down, then continue on their way. The little house near by stood mostly empty.

The large climbing frame with netting and rope ladders was used by boys 7 -10 who climbed, lay and talked in the netting, or chased each other around. Younger children have climbed up the ladders, hung by their knees, and sometimes sat in the netting.

The ping pong table was never used for playing ping-pong during the time we were observing, but occasionally children climbed up on it and jumped around.

How the surfaces were used.

Bike riding was by far the most popular activity. The stone pavement and the small asphalt surfaces surrounding the play area were constantly used for cycling by children up to the age of seven. Sometimes even older children cycled here, frequently on bikes belonging to younger children. There is a notice that bike riding, ball playing, soccer and hockey are forbidden in the area. As far as bike riding goes, it seems at least in practice that tricycle and small bikes are an exception. Children are very much aware of this rule even though they break it. A group of boys was observed one time playing hockey on a part of the paved area. But for the most part those who wanted to play soccer and such games went to Tessin park. The paved area was also used for pushing doll buggies and, in general, as an outdoor meeting place. In particular, people gathered in front of the center passageway, including adults now and then. They sat on the edge of the planters or remained standing. This place is sunny and, being centrally located, provides a certain vantage point from which to watch what is going on in other parts of the yard. The difference between sunny and shady areas is very marked, both in terms of light and warmth. The sunny areas feel much friendlier.

The plants are used to some extent, when in leaf, to hide behind and sneak along. It has happened that children have broken off branches or picked leaves to use in their play. One three-year-old girl "planted" a branch in the sand-pit. Access to "litter" is limited except for what can be found in the trash containers.

To change - to destroy?

There is hardly any chance for a child to change the playground in any way himself, other than by bringing along his own toys. Only the usual pails, shovels, dolls, wagons, small cars, bikes and other such toys were seen.

The only change occurring, while we were making our observations was that the netting of the large climbing frame got a hole in it. This was of interest to children 7 -10 who tried to see if they could wriggle through the hole!

In our opinion, the playground at Faltoversten functions more as a "place to pass through" than as a place for concentrated and absorbing play. The inadequacies have more to do with basic planning mistakes than the selection of play equipment. As long as a housing complex is made up of long, high buildings so that the play areas lie in the shade most of the day, the outdoor environment cannot be attractive. Nor does the use of only right angles and stiff design in the open areas do anything to alleviate the impression of coldness.

Brandbergen

Residential area

Brandbergen is a bedroom community located in Haninge township, a 25-minute commute by train from the center of Stockholm. The area consists of cooperative apartment buildings constructed by HSB (the National Association of Tenants' Savings and Building Societies).

People we talked to in the area said that the apartments are very nice and well-planned. Since they are tenant-owned, the residents have a chance to decide on paints and wallpaper, and we noticed that many balconies were painted in individual ways. It can be difficult, however, to sell one's apartment, and HSB therefore advertises that some of the apartments include a repurchase guarantee. Parents we met at the playground said that there are many who want to sell their apartments but cannot. Young families are clearly in the majority, and there are many Finnish immigrants living in the area. It is hard to get a place in a day-care center, and the fees are high. There are only two supervised play parks in the town of Handen, and none in Brandbergen. People's lives are very much affected by the long distance to town. There are few jobs to be had in the immediate vicinity.

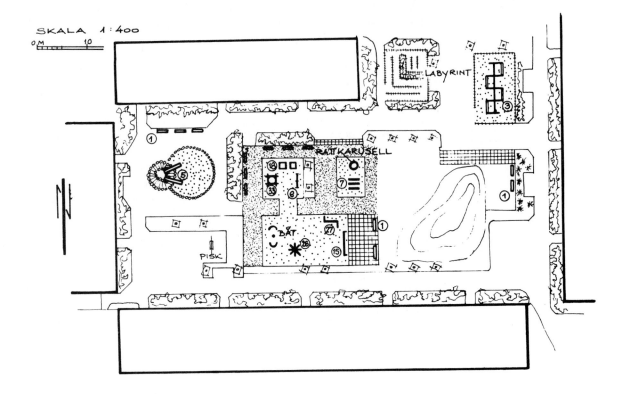

Design of the playground.

The playground gives an impression of flatness. It is rectangular in shape and relatively large, about 5,000 square meters. On three sides it is bounded by three-story buildings and on the fourth by an eight-story building. The housing area was constructed on a flat rock plateau, where most of the vegetation had already burned down (hence its name: Brandbergen means "fire rock"). So there were few natural features to preserve. The playground is entirely man-made. In some of the other play areas in the district there is a tree or a rocky outcrop, but not in the one we observed. Most of the space is taken up by two large sand-pits, and low climbing apparatus is spread out over the entire sand area. Of the fourteen pieces of play equipment present, eight are intended to be used by younger children for climbing. At each end of the yard an attempt has been made to achieve some degree of variety by means of a three-meter-high artificial grassy hill at one end and a terraced mound with smooth asphalt surface to which two narrow slides have been attached at the other end. Next to the grassy hill is a section with ten swings, all with fabric slings as seats, half of them designed for small children. Next to the swings is a maze formed with fencing. The area around the playground up to the entrance is paved with asphalt.

Stiff and monotonous

The play equipment is laid out completely symmetrically. The area gives the impression of having just been tidied up and is planned very much from a typical adult point of view. All the wooden climbing poles are the same height and the same distance apart. The other equipment is also set out at equal intervals. No attempt has been made to group the facilities so that they can be played with together. Balance beams and ropes fill no particular function, since they do not lead from one place to another. The maze has no dead-ends so that it is impossible to get lost. Only one of the three sand-pits in the yard is free of equipment, except that the slides end there.

No sheltered places

All the vegetation here, as in the rest of the area, has been planted; it is very sparse and does not help to define distinct areas. There are no full-grown trees, but here and there a tree about three meters high. The grass on the hill is worn-looking. The playground is sunny but lacks any protection from the sun, wind or rain. The place is quite windy because of the way the buildings are arranged; there is **always** a draught even when it is completely still elsewhere. There is no calm, sheltered spot for children or grown-ups to sit.

Nearly all the children and grown-ups disappear when it rains. The playground affords no chance to experience an "indoors" outdoors. Despite this, it does happen now and then that children stay out in the rain, or that a mother waits in the entry in the hope that the rain will soon be over, while the children play in the doorway.

All the soil had to be brought in since Brandbergen was bare rock. The "soil" is really hardened clay (below).

Asphalt, sand and low climbing equipment, a place to play?

It is the asphalt, grass and sand which get the most use by far (over 70% of the time children are at the playground). See appendix I.

Small children want to be close to grown-ups.

Few grown-ups

Most of those living in the area are families with preschool children. The area is full of children. Since it is difficult to make child-care arrangements, many mothers stay at home. Despite this, we saw few grown-ups outdoors. There was a group of about five mothers and sometimes a father present on various occasions. These parents seemed to have a good relationship among themselves and they sat on the benches talking together. Other mothers have sat alone. Only in the mornings have there been grown-ups out. The grown-ups, almost without exception, sat on the benches near the small play houses since the shrubbery has grown up somewhat there. Occasionally they have sat on the asphalt and sunned themselves.

On one occasion, when the popular bench was fully occupied, a mother sat with her **back** against the bench and with her child in front of her in the sand. On the same occasion, another mother, also sat with her back turned toward the other mothers. This somewhat strange position gave the impression that these two mothers felt a need to be apart with their children both for their own sake and to avoid obtruding on the group sitting and talking on the bench.

These grown-ups surely would enjoy themselves more outdoors if they did not have to use their backs as a "wall."

The presence of grown-ups definitely influences the children's play

When there have been adults out, the children have clustered around them. On one occasion a mother moved from the bench to the wooden poles in the sand, with the result that not only her own children but other children and mothers (!) seated themselves near by and the sand, the poles and even the edges of the sand-pit were well used! Mothers, in other words, stimulate and restrict the use of certain equipment by their mere presence. We have even seen examples of more active interference, as when a girl of about two went into the maze (which can perhaps provide some excitement at this age) and her mother rushed forward immediately and moved her to the sand-pit where she could keep an eye on her. Once in the autumn there were some small children in one if the houses, and pinching and yelling ensued. Since the mothers could not see the children there at the same time that they remained on the bench (the entry of the house being on the other side), the children were taken out and put in the sand-pit.

Only parents of small children have stayed outside. Most of the time, the only adults to be seen were there just passing by. The children have shown a great interest in contact with adults. Besides residents, a garbage collector and a mailman (a woman) have passed by. When the mailman came, the children greeted and followed her. When the garbage collector came, they stopped playing in the sand and ran after him, picking up litter and putting it in his cart. The children have been very interested in talking to the observer. They have spontaneously started explaining how they would like things to be in the play area and how it was at the beginning. Several of the younger children have been hard to "shake off" and have faithfully followed along and asked about what we were doing. This marked interest was in contrast to what the observers encountered in other supervised and unsupervised playgrounds.

Conflicts among children

On several occasions fighting broke out. Children threw clumps of dirt at each other or ganged up against each other. The psychological climate in the yard could be very harsh at times especially for the younger children. When there was trouble these children often turned to the observer, since there was seldom any other grown-up present. On several occasions younger children became frightened by the fighting and went in crying, or simply kept quiet. A few of the older children, especially the leaders of the gangs, were irritated by the presence of the observer ("she's not going to mix into our business"), and others were afraid that the observer would write down that they had been throwing mud and that HSB would find out about it. To these children, HSB seemed to be an intimidating power that could punish "naughty" children rather than an association which could help see to it that children had better things to do than throw mud at each other.

Nowhere to be

The neighborhood is full of children who are at home. Still, the playground has few visitors. It is natural to assume that this is because the

playground is so boring. This assumption is confirmed by the children we have talked to. The older children feel like they have nowhere to play ball. Despite the relatively large size, children feel they do not have enough room! One boy, 7 - 10 years old, spoke dreamily about how nice it would be if it could be like the place where he goes to spend the summer. "There they have a large lawn and they can do whatever they want . . . and build huts . . . and they have trees this big!" He described them with words and gestures and then suddenly exclaimed, "Here there aren't any trees!" The boy's friend said he would like "a big house where you can hoist yourself up and then let go and land in masses of foam rubber . . . and a bicycle course would be nice."

A corner to oneself

As far as younger children go, our observations of them at play in the sand indicate that they never make use of the entire or even of a large part of the sand-pit, but often keep to the corners. This is surely evidence of the need for a cozy spot of one's own, a nook cut off from the activities and view of others. Even older children use just a portion of the equipment-filled sand-pits. The sand around the swings and at the bottom of the slides has been used for building large connected constructions as well as for wrestling and jumping. Once in the autumn two boys, ages 7 - 10, used the area between the two playhouses and the edge of the sand-pit for building forts and playing war.

When it comes to sand-pits, it seems that younger children have a greater feeling of spaciousness the more secluded nooks and corners they can find, especially if these are near a place where grown-ups like to sit. For bigger children, spaciousness means sand areas that are open, that is, free of fixed equipment, preferably cut off somewhat from other children and adults so that imaginative play can develop without being disturbed by others. Our observations indicate that children often played, for example, next to the asphalt mound or **behind** the grassy hill or small playhouses.

At this playground, nooks and corners are very hard to find. Once a boy suggested playing hide-and-go-seek, something which aroused the observer's curiosity very much. The children hid behind the grassy hillock, but the game soon died out. There simply were not enough hiding places. This is above all due to the vegetation being so sparse.

Our observations also indicate that **all** the children at the playground often gather in one place. For example, everyone who is present sits in the swings or in the sand around them. One time all the children gathered around three boys, ages 3-5, who were playing with excavators in the sand. Another time everyone gathered around the carousel, which someone had covered with a thick layer of sand. On other occasions all the children collected around a hole which they had made in the grassy hill, or in the maze.

It happens very infrequently at this playground that a small group of children are able to play undisturbed by others. There is so little going on, and so few secluded spots, where something is happening. This leads, if not to fighting, then at lease to a situation in which the majority of children are

Playing is best when children can play undisturbed in small groups.

just on-lookers. It is naturally those who are small or passive or less tough who just look. Despite the large size, this playground is **not** experienced as spacious.

The asphalt is used for many things, above all for riding bikes.

In a pitted, not too carefully paved area, water puddles are formed which encourage exploration and play.

How the play equipment
and surfaces were used

The playground is largely taken up with fixed play equipment intended for younger children - but rarely used by children of any age.

That which attracts children to the playground is above all the chance to meet others. Grass, flower beds, gravel, sand, asphalt and swings are used most. It is here children were to be found most of the time, 88% in the autumn and 85% in the spring. Equipment other than swings and sand-pits were used little (12% in the autumn, 15% in the spring). What draws the children away from the playground is primarily the chance to ride bikes through the entire shopping area of Brandbergen. There are playgrounds in every courtyard in the area, all full of equipment. Variation among these play areas is, however, limited, so there is no special reason to visit "the neighbor's yard."

Girls from 7 - 10 say that they like best to swing, turn somersaults, and hop twist. However they have trouble finding a place to hop twist. The best place is the carpet-beating rack which lies outside the play area and where they can play three-corner twist. In the spring, the most common activities among girls were, besides hopping twist, playing hop-scotch, jumping rope and taking small children for a stroll. The boys rode bikes and played soccer

This carpet-beating rack is good for hopping twist.

or cowboys and indians. The children play mostly in the few free open spaces that are "left over", using loose materials they have brought with them.

Dreaming of change

We have said earlier that the children did not seem to feel any sense of participation in the tenant-owners' association to which their parents belong. Nor do they seem to feel that they can have an influence in deciding how their play area is designed. One boy sighed and said how nice it was when he first moved in. "At that time none of this stuff was here. Everything was in a terrible mess and we used to make trouble for the construction workers. In the evening we used to have a fire with mother and dad and some others that had also just moved in. But we never do that now. It used to be a lot more fun (pointing to the asphalt mound) before they built that thing there. Then everything lay scattered about and we climbed on the stuff and built forts. Now it's no fun anymore . . . It was the same before they had finished making the grass hill." A girl about the same age explained a little hesitantly, like she was afraid of sounding ungrateful, "We have already done everything here. We know how to do it. So it's not so much fun any more."

To change - to make a mess?

The yard is entirely lacking in play materials which can be altered. The only thing the children can change and create with is the sand, the soil in the planters, and any bit of litter they happen to find. It is very common for children to play in the sand. The make roads, tunnels, forts, pits. As already mentioned, one day the children covered the carousel with a thick layer of sand. On several occasions they played war using lumps of dirt. The walls around some of the doorways were covered with dry mud. The children had managed to change the grassy hill by enlarging a hole caused while sliding on it during the winter. The hole was very popular. Children pretended to trip over it, sat in it and fought over whose it was. The children soon made another hole near the first one.

The only loose material at the playground has been litter. Once in the autumn two boys, ages 3- 5, found a cardboard box and they jumped into it and rolled around in the sand. They played energetically, laughing tremendously, until a bigger boy came and took the box away from them. The small boys gave up the fight over the box with a sigh. During the autumn and spring there was a grocery cart standing in the yard. The children rode on it and pushed each other around. Otherwise the children kept busy with loose materials brought from home, above all bicycles. Mothers of small children brought buckets, shovels and cars along. Older children had pistols and indian outfits, small cars, jump ropes, stones for playing hopscotch, and balls.

One windy day the children made "Kites" from plastic bags.

*At the top of the hill, the wind caught
hold of them!*

Mine and yours

One sign that the playground is perhaps not regarded as "mine" by the children is that they seldom leave their toys behind. In the spring an old bucket was left outside for about two weeks. Otherwise, both children and adults were very careful about taking everything back inside with them. Several parents we talked to said that there were a group af children living there who never brought along anything to play with when they came out, even though their mothers were at home. These children rushed up as soon as one of the "other" mothers came out and asked if they could borrow shovels and cars. When these mothers had to go in, the children kindly returned what they had borrowed.

Somewhere to be

The harsh psychological climate and the lack of adult involvement, together with the lack of variety, all have a negative effect on how much the playground is used. Another factor that decreases use even further is the absence of any shelter against sun, wind or rain. Furthermore, natural meeting places are lacking outdoors and there is no indoor facility with access to staff and materials. The chance for these deficiencies to be remedied while the children in the area are still young is in one sense favorable, since several apartments are vacant, especially on the ground floor. From an economic point of view, however, improvement is doubtful since the

township is hard-pressed financially. Nevertheless, it has been possible to find good solutions to similar problems in other areas, as for exemple in Rosengård in Malmö where someone living in the area has been employed as a play leader several hours a day and where the responsibility for looking after the facilities have little by little been handed over to the residents themselves (see Insulander, E, 1975).

We see, then, that the lack of alternatives and the absence of cozy nooks and corners and sheltered spots means that the playground does not function well either for children or for adults. It is worth pausing for a moment, before turning to a description of another unsupervised playground, to consider another park which functions quite differently.

In Hallonbergen, a suburb of Stockholm, there is a supervised play park which lies at the foot of a hill on a flat surface. The physical conditions are not particularly promising in many respects. Nevertheless, this park offers a positive experience to both children and mothers. Everyone seems to enjoy themselves, the place is full of life and action. The mothers often have with them juice and coffee, rolls and cookies, and even baby food. Those who come stay a long time, go home only to eat, and then come back. There is a fine place for adults to sit, with benches and a nice table. Attractively screened off, it provides a few moments of peace and quiet, but is also near the swings, sand-pit and playhouses. There is a feeling of coziness about the park and mothers and children feel that it is "theirs."

One distinguishing feature of this park is that it promotes many different activities for many different age-groups at the same time. The screened-off areas contribute to this. Children can continue with what they are doing relatively undisturbed; they are not distracted or interrupted all the time by what others are doing.

The need adults have to relate to each other can easily collide with children's insistence on attention and supervision. An attractive outdoor environment can provide a chance to relax and talk with others.

The play park has a number of tricycles which are in constant use. When these large tricycles were new, a waiting list was necessary.

We have noticed that when children use bikes or wagons, they often make a little "tour" of the park. They ride around the fireplace, past the chest of building blocks and the ping-pong table, turn at the bike carousel onto the path that runs along the soccer field, then go in toward the asphalt square again. During such a tour they see everything that is going on in the various parts of the park. They often stop a while and watch what others are doing. Sometimes such a tour is part of a game, such as going for a bus ride. The children often chase each other around the park, screaming loudly.

To compare a supervised play park with an unsupervised local playground is of course like comparing night and day. The mere fact that at a play park children can borrow loose materials has a strong positive effect on play. Still, there are unsupervised playgrounds which function better than those considered so far. We turn to several of these now.

Tingvalla
Residential area

This playground is on Tingvallavägen in Märsta, a suburb north of Stockholm about 30 minutes away by commuter train, and close to Märsta Center. The large apartment building adjacent to this play area is very different from the surrounding buildings. It is high, long, gently curved and painted with bright colors. The playground is furnished with a lot of fixed equipment. The apartment buildings lying behind this area are slightly

curved and only three stories high, and the playgrounds there are much less well-equipped. The large apartment building is managed by Stiftelsen Sigtunahem and the residents have certain special tenant rights.

Design of the playground

Previously, the playground was quite barren, but during the past year it has been fixed up and furnished with play equipment intended for children up to the age of twelve. In addition, there is room for various kinds of ball games, like land hockey, soccer and ping-pong, activities which can attract adults as well as children. The playground includes a spacious, gently sloping grass area in front of the large apartment building. In front of the building itself, and encircling the lawn, is an asphalt path. There are also paths crossing the lawn.

A natural hill with some full-grown trees and bushes screens off the play area somewhat from the near-by street with its traffic. There is a fence to keep smaller children from going out onto the road. The little hill with trees was at one time nearly the only place where children could play. Now there is a look-out tower on it. Play equipment is set out in "groups" all over the large grass area, with sand beneath. Besides the look-out tower there are two large playhouses, three plastic cubes of various heights, a small combination climbing house and slide, a small playhouse with roof, a storefront, a large climbing apparatus with netting, rope ladders and ropes, a playhouse built of logs without a door and with a sand floor, an aerial ropeway, swings, a tractor-tire swing and two large sand-pits. Furthermore,

The playhouse is used mostly to climb on. Its location right next to the climbing frame discourage quiet imaginative play.

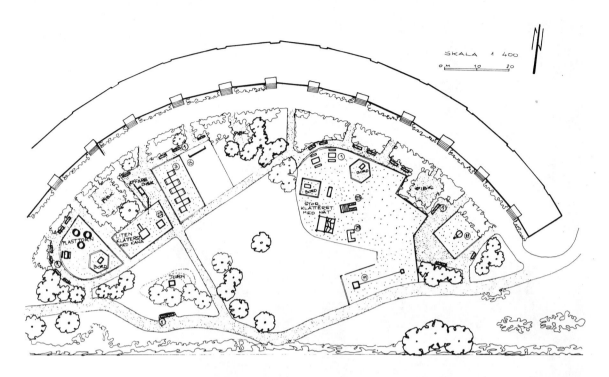

there is a ping-pong table, a back-board with an asphalt surface in front of it, and two soccer goals in the grass. Most of the "play equipment groups" have benches near by, and in some places there are also tables. The playground is sunny, with normal wind conditions. There is no shelter from wind or rain except for the playhouses. Bushes have been planted but have not yet grown much.

Children "take care of themselves"

As a local playground Tingvalla must be regarded as easily accessible. No car traffic is allowed in the yard, so that even younger children can play outside without direct supervision. Very few adults are seen outdoors, presumably because it is possible to see the children from balconies and windows. Another reason for so few adults may be that the play area is so open and exposed. It has a certain "backyard" character due to the curvature of the building and to the hill, which acts somewhat as a screen, but anyone sitting on the grass or on the benches is in full view of others. There are no secluded corners.

On one occasion in the spring a few grown-ups came out to sun themselves and they chose to lie behind a shrub at some distance from the house. On the same occasion, some children (5 - 6 boys) preferred to play soccer on the lawn in front of the adults instead of using the goals provided.

Contact between adults seemed to consist primarily of meetings on the way to or from the apartment building, when people would stand talking for a few minutes. On several occasions we observed parents com-

municating with their children through the windows. This form of contact is difficult in a multi-story building, however, and it is very seldom that a child called up to a grown-up. No activity among the children was observed to be either stimulated or prevented by the parents. If there were adults present at the playground, they usually came from another part of the area. They brought their children here because there are so many different types of play equipment available. It is easy to tell which children are "just visiting." They dash about from one piece of equipment to the next, five of discovering what there is to do.

In the morning only a few children were at the playground, usually two to five of preschool age. As a rule the same few children were out every day, regardless of weather. In the afternoon the number of children varied depending on weather but was usually about 15 - 20 after school finished. The ages of the children then ranged from 3 to 15. The younger children had older sisters and brothers looking after them. The children who play here in the afternoon come mostly from the adjacent building and they know each other. Conflicts involving children pushing or hitting each other occur rather often without any apparent reason. These do not last long, however, and after a short time the children resume playing together as if nothing had happened. Immigrant children play together with Swedish children and there is no split between these two groups.

How the play equipment was used

The playground's "own" children did not show the same curiosity about the equipment as did the "visitors." They can manage the equipment, have already found out what there is to do, and have no opportunity to change anything. Because the equipment is so static, it is soon "used up" and the children lose interest. Of the fixed equipment, it was the large climbing frame that was used most by school-age children. Lively games like tag dominated and the roof of the timbered house near by was often used for crawling on. We never saw the playhouse being used for imaginative play, which can be due in part to the fact that it is so close to the climbing apparatus that it is hard to play undisturbed there. The small combination climbing house was used primarily by younger children. They went down the slide, climbed around, swung and played house.

How the surfaces were used

Both younger and older children spent most of their time on the footpaths. They rode around on bikes, and often stood talking close to the building and next to the steps. That they stayed so close to home can be due partly to a feeling of being safe there, and partly to the fact that adults pass by there. Little happens at the playground. Several boys who tried to get a moped started, for example, attracted the attention of all the other children, of every age, one entire afternoon. The only adult we have seen doing any work in the area was the caretaker, but the children were not especially interested in him.

Sex role differences show up early. Still, soccer is exciting!

It is important that a playground have many different kinds of surfaces. This area is much used for soccer and land hockey in the autumn.

The lawn was used quite a lot, especially for kicking a ball around in the spring, and also for romping about and picking flowers. In the autumn, land hockey was by far the most popular rule game, and the asphalt surface in front of the backboard was used for this. Even though this asphalt surface is not large, it seems to function very well and was used by boys up to the age of 15. It was also possible to play ping-pong, but during the time we made our observations no one did so.

The sand-pits were used a great deal by both younger and older children. As in most other playgrounds, sand is one of the few materials that it is possible to create something from. Access to natural materials which can be used in playing is limited, as at most places. On one occasion some children broke off branches from a planted bush to use as arrows. This led to a big fight, since other children rightly pointed out that it was forbidden to break off branches.

Taking things out

There is quite a lot of equipment in the playground that is meant to be used in imaginative play. For such play to develop, children need to have loose items available, like buckets and dishes, cloths and dress-up clothes. Since this is a local play area which children experience as their own, they take out a lot of things, particularly bikes, buckets, doll wagons, and small odds and ends, and they often leave them out until the next day. One morning we watched two girls, 5 - 6 years old, playing store for more than an hour at the store-front, one of the few occasions when this piece of equipment was used. They rode around on their bikes and gathered things from the trash containers (cans and bottles) to sell in their store. The girls were very much aware that these things were considered "junk" and disliked by grown-ups.

Need for variety

Even though their own yard offers so many kinds of equipment, the children sometimes go to other, sparsely-equipped yards near by for change and variation. They are attracted by the baby swings, where they can swing their dolls without them tumbling off, a free-standing low slide with a bump in it, and a worn-out carousel.

Tingvalla is a playground that makes a considerably more mellow impression than Fältöversten or Brandbergen. The selection of fixed equipment has been made more carefully in the sense that there has been an effort to satisfy the needs of both younger and older children. Equipment for imaginative play has been included, even though the results are not particularly

When the environment is too-tidy, with no sticks, cones, leaves or other "litter" around, there is nothing to sell and the store remains unused.

successful. We feel that the surfaces and some of the equipment function well, but despite this Tingvalla suffers from many of the same shortcomings found in most playgrounds today. Meaningful adult activity is missing, as well as secluded corners and access to loose materials. The local playgrounds that function best are those which are situated near low houses, whether multi- or single-family. One example from a multi-family area is Bellman.

Bellman
Residential area

The residential area is located on the outskirts of the city of Uppsala. Bellman is a tenant-owners' society with 400 cooperative apartments. The first residents moved in in 1968. The area consists of three low buildings set at right angles to each other so that they form a courtyard within. There are three such sections, each with the same design of buildings and courtyard. We have observed the middle yard. Families with children predominate; there are about 400 children living here. The area is fairly attractive and people seem happy to remain. Day-care centers, schools and services are all near by.

All the playgrounds in the area have gotten a thorough face-lifting since 1973. The initiative for this came from the residents themselves, and the Play Council helped with the planning (Residential environment for children, Play Council, 1 December 1973). According to its report, "the Play Council presented a planning suggestion at the request of a group within the resident's organization. The suggestion was revised somewhat by the group and it was then decided to divide the work up into various stages." Stage I involved replacing dead plants with new ones, making safety improvements, removing old equipment and adding new equipment, and rearranging the play surfaces, including making a carpentry area and building some grassy mounds. Stage II was to consist of removing all dangerous and poisonous plants, expanding the carpentry area and producing play equipment themselves. "The goal of the Play Council and the residents' group was to create an environment which would be stimulating for both chilren and grown-ups, so that children would be happy to stay within the protected housing area."

All the buildings look the same, between the houses and around the yards are straight paths. The whole area is flat, with grass in all three courtyards. The three play areas have, however, been given different characters by varying the equipment in them. In addition, the mounds built up in the yards each have a somewhat different shape and location.

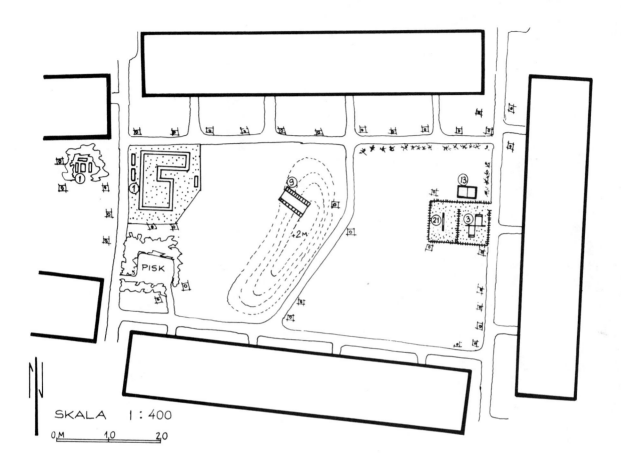

Bellman

Design of the playground

The playground we observed has a slide fixed to the mound in the middle of the grassy area. At one end there is a wooden house, swings (baby swings and tire swings) and a tractor-tire swing, all with sand beneath. It is here that the carpentry area is to be located and boards began arriving during the course of the spring. On the other side are a sand-pit and somersault bar. In the autumn and for a while in the spring there was a peak-house and a climbing tree in the sand. These were later removed. A high-jump with a mat was added in the spring. There are movable benches which are usually placed next to the sand-pit and the wooden house, as well as bench-tables for children.

Vegetation

Shrubbery has grown up around the buildings and the carpetbeating rack. That planted after the alterations has not yet grown up. Adjacent to the observed play area there is an open grassy area which can be used, for example, to play croquet. There is also a circular arbor (newly planted) where tables and benches are to be placed in the summer.

Equipment in neighboring yards

The two yards on either side also have sand-pits and swings but otherwise they have deliberately been equipped somewhat differently. In one a look-out tower on a hill and a roofed-over sand-pit predominate. There is also a grill. The other yard has an aerial ropeway which starts from a mound.

The usual swings have been supplemented with a tractor-tire swing. The grassy mound divides up the playground and is nice for sledding in the winter.

The security of everyone knowing each other

The play area is exposed to wind, but it is sunny. It is right outside the entry doors, no cars are allowed, and it feels safe to go out where everyone knows each other. Children as young as three can be out alone. There is no equipment which is dangerous and the low height of the buildings makes it possible for parents to keep an eye on their children from the windows. The younger children stay put in the courtyard.

Since the houses are built to form a square, the playground is an enclosed area, but the low buildings keep it from feeling too closed-in. Paths and buildings are straight, but within the courtyard itself, there are certain forms which break up the monotony. The man-made mound is irregular, the sand-pit is asymmetrical, and a circular lilac hedge is planted next to the play area. These are only small details, to be sure, but still they are noticeable and help to provide a little variety. Since the courtyards are somewhat differently designed, this also creates variety in the area as a whole. The older children can visit the neighboring yards and do different things than they can do in their own yard. Still, children clearly experience this playground as "theirs." If children from other parts of the housing complex come in, someone can occasionally be heard to say, "You're not allowed to play in our yard!"

The playground is fairly large, wide, and might seem desolate at times were it not for the mound that divides up the space. A number of different activities can go on at the same time without disturbing each other, so that the playground feels spacious.

The playground is used most by children
from the surrounding houses

Most of the children present are from three to seven years old. All children know each other, so it is easy to find someone to play with. The smaller children are comforted by the older ones if they get hurt. The very youngest are also helped with what they cannot manage themselves, such as getting up on the swings. Normally there are few adults out unless the weather is fine. A child maintains close contact with his mother through the window, and mothers call to their children if they want something. Very often children stood and shouted to a grown-up for help with some trifling or serious problem. The parents seemed able to keep up quite well with what was happening, and they knew all the children. In general children did not call out in vain, but were answered. The number of children present varied of course with the weather, but not so much as at playgrounds farther from home. When the weather was good, there were from 10 - 20 children out at one time. From the age of five on, boys mostly played with boys and girls with girls. Minor conflicts occurred now and then, but nothing serious.

The grown-ups around were mostly mothers, and the contacts between them were lively. Several times they drank coffee out on the grass. Grown-ups seldom participated directly in the children's activities, but they kept a watchful eye on them. We did not notice that any particular activity was prevented or encouraged.

How the play equipment was used

Of all the equipment, the sand-pits were used most. Since there are two sand areas, slightly bigger children have a chance to play undisturbed. That the peak-house and the climbing-tree disappeared from the sand-pit did not seem to have any negative effect. On the contrary, there was more space afterwards in the sand and this provided greater opportunities to build roads and even whole cities. The children brought with them pails, shovels, cake tins and cars. On one occasion we saw three boys play with cars very intensively for a half-hour. They built roads in the whole sand-pit, set up small sticks as bars that had to be opened in order to pass, and fixed up parking lots for guest cars. Then they all took turns pretending to have a birthday party, and it was very important that the guests parked their cars properly. Afterwards they sang "Happy Birthday" to each other.

Another place where children often played with their cars was in the bushes around the carpet-beating rack. They made winding, twisting tracks there and crawled around on their hands and knees racing their cars.

The slide was very popular and it happened that even big children came and used it for a little while. The slide is wide and children can go down it in many different ways. The wooden house with projecting roof (a module) was used in imaginative and role games like mother-father-child, baker, and

• *When the slide is fixed to a grassy slope, children can go up and down at their own pace. The risk of accidents is less and small children can play too.*

• *A cozy little nook is needed at every playground.*

A simple structure like this can serve many play purposes, providing chances for climbing, experiencing heights, and even turning upside down.

store. It functioned even as a climbing apparatus for boys and girls up to the age of seven. Competition over the swings sometimes occurred since there is only one tire swing and one baby swing. This did not, however, express itself in hostility but rather in teasing. The child or children (often two swung together) who succeeded in getting to the swing first sang or yelled triumphantly while swinging. The large tractor-tire swing did not arouse the same degree of interest among children up to six, but older children used it some, often for sitting and chatting.

How the surfaces were used

The asphalt paths and grass areas were well used. The paths served mainly for biking, pulling wagons, pushing doll buggies and jumping rope. The grass surfaces and grassy mound were used for running and tumbling. Once a gang of 5 - 7-year-old boys was observed playing war on the mound. One pretended to strike, and the others rolled down the hill.

When a high-jump frame arrived at the playground, older children, ages 10 - 15, showed up. Even though it rained very hard at times that afternoon, the drawing power of the new equipment was so great that children stayed out anyway and played on it. Such strong interest was of course largely because it was new. At other playgrounds where high-jump equipment has been available longer, however, it has continued to be popular among older children. Even the younger children enjoyed using it. In the morning they would stand in line for a turn to jump and tumble about on the mat.

Right up to the final day of the observation period, the playground was used primarily by children up to the age of seven, and rarely by children over ten. Few older children were seen, and according to what we heard, children 10 - 12 felt they did not have anything to do. There is a soccer field at the near-by school, but the children felt it was too far to go there. People in the area were discussing the idea of adding a gravel field or a tennis court.

To change - to create?

The equipment available is static and cannot be altered. If a carpentry corner becomes a reality, then it will give both older and younger children in the area a chance for creative activity.

Somewhere to be

There is no secluded place where adults or children can meet, but this may change when the circular hedge grows higher. There is a grill in the next yard for having parties together. Since many of the adults know each other, people simply meet and talk on the lawn. Mothers (as is most often the case) sit mostly on the benches by the wooden house, probably because small children have the most to do there (sand, house, swings). It is also a bit cozy, since the buildings form a corner there. When children were enjoying quiet games, such as playing with dolls, they often sat on the grass near the walls of the houses.

The strongest positive factors contributing to the way play functions at Bellman are probably the good feelings that exist among people living in the area, and the shared experience of working together to improve their environment. Cooperation was made easier by the fact that the area was formerly student housing, so that many of the residents have similar backgrounds and friendships come about naturally. The low buildings and the manageable size of the area makes it easier for children to get to know each other and for grown-ups to share responsibility for them.

Another place where we find the same sense of security, and closeness to nature as well, is the single-family housing area of Sandvik in Viksjó.

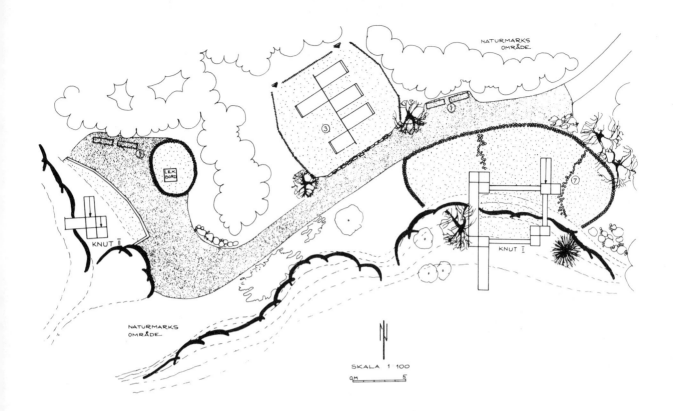

"The Knot" is one of the few kinds of equipment that small children can climb on with safety.

Sandvik

Residential area

Sandvik is a single-family housing area in Viksjö in Järfälla township, developed during the 1970s. (For a closer look at the planning process and what it is like for children to live in small private houses, see Uno Dahlén, 1977). The area has different types of houses for families of different sizes. It is hilly and situated close to a wooded rocky slope. A traffic-free path leads to near-by Viksjö Center. In Viksjö there are few day-care center places and hardly any jobs.

Design of the playgrounds

The two playgrounds which we observed in Sandvik lie on either side of a rocky outcrop. In addition to swings and sand-pit, there is only one type of equipment, called "the knot." This consists of platforms of various sizes which can be mounted at different heights depending on what is wanted and on the terrain. The platforms can be complemented with steps, suspension-bridges and slides. (For a further description, see Appendix 3.)

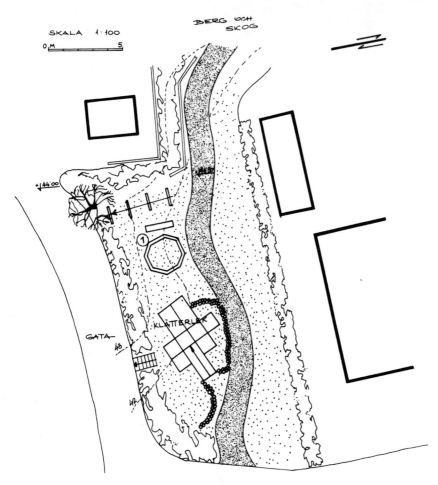

In order to get an understanding of how the playground as a whole functions, we have recorded what children do in this entire section of the housing area, even on the paths, in the surrounding open space, in the garages and up in the woods.

To be where something is going on

As far as accessibility is concerned, the playgrounds are well-planned. The larger playground is situated between the houses and the natural area, which means that children are tempted to use nature in their play. The smaller playground is centrally located in a place where many adults and children pass by and readily stop. Those who visit the larger playground do so more by plan, and they stay longer also. This holds true, however, mostly for parents with small children. Children ages five and up use this playground also "on the run." One mother told us that she goes to the larger playground mostly because it is the only place in the area where there are swings. She thinks it is a pity that there are no swings at the smaller playground.

The houses push nearly up into the woods and hills. The play equipment is situated so that it melts in with the surroundings.

One thing which contributes very much to the playground's being not so well attended is the fact that the area as a whole contains so many other places for children to play. During our observation time, it was the gently sloping asphalt surfaces between the garages and the paths in front of the houses that were used most. On one occasion, all the playgrounds were empty during most of the observation period, although there were many children outside. The majority of children played on the asphalt between the garages where they rode bikes over a sand pile next to somebody's yard. The children got up as much speed as possible, zoomed over the sand pile, and "flew" a bit on the other side. A number of children gathered around to watch. The play continued energetically for several hours. On several other occasions as well the children kept to this area.

They rode round and round on their bikes, used pedal cars, tricycles, tractors, carts and doll buggies, or just walked around. Interesting things sometimes happen on the asphalt paths. A man cleaning out drains attracted great attention; for 45 minutes he was closely watched by six children. They commented: "It smells like at the beach." "It doesn't matter if I get splashed since I have glasses on." "You stop for lunch later, huh?

The question is if children need more climbing opportunities than this. Here all movements are possible in a natural setting.

To gather speed and then ride over a sand pile was an exciting game that drew children away from the playgrounds.

Workers get a lunch break.'' The man won out over all the play facilities in the area. When the garbage truck came, there were also a faithful audience.

The housing area is not entirely dominated by young women and children, as so many newly-built areas are. Some older women with dogs of various sizes have gone past, and some men as well. The fact that something can happen, that people pass on bikes or on foot, increases the attraction of the asphalt paths a great deal.

The children living here also have a chance to play in their own yards, and this happens. Children have been observed playing in their own sandbox or cycling or playing ball on their own paths. In most cases a group of children have played together. This means that children go visiting in each other's yards.

Mine and yours

It is obvious that the feeling of "we" is very strong in this area and that children experience the playgrounds as "theirs." Several times playthings have been left out on the playground: "Sara's bike", "Kicki's gun", a plastic car, some buckets. Once a mother tossed all the playthings left behind at the smaller playground into the neighboring yard, where she no doubt felt they were safer. Children have also left their creations in the sand-pit. One morning there were two fine pies there, decorated with gravel, sticks and bright yellow dandelions.

Somewhere to meet

The playgrounds serve as important meeting places, not least for mothers in the area. On several occasions as many as six mothers gathered in the smaller playground and carried on a lively conversation with one another. The swing area in the larger playground also seems to function as a meeting place. The mothers sit on the simple, uncomfortable fence, push their children and talk with each other. The benches remain empty. One time

A sand-pit which goes all the way up to a rocky hill stimulates the imagination. The edge can resemble a beach, the rocks can be used for baking cakes or playing with cars. It is interesting to bang with a shovel and discover that the wooden planks and the rocks make different sounds.

there were five mothers with their children there. One of them read while the others talked. One child wanted to go home, but her mother preferred to stay. "You and I are home all the time..." The girl reluctantly stayed, but she would rather have gone home to **play.**

The area offers opportunities both for contact and for privacy. Seclusion is found in one's own yard and up in the hills and woods. It must be regarded as an obvious advantage that both children and adults have this chance to choose. We can state that children in Sandvik have a varied and secure play environment.

It is on the asphalt surfaces that the most things happen. Adults pass by, someone packs up a car and drives away, the garbage truck comes, people meet.

Still, this area has one important negative feature in common with all the other areas we have described. Children are by themselves for the most part. They are relegated to special places far from the everyday adult world, where they are to stay until they are considered "useful" to society. Where are the models for them to copy, the diversified adult life, the involvement and sharing of responsibility? We have seen that a grown-up at work holds an enormous fascination for these children. Such a person is unfortunately almost unique in their environment.

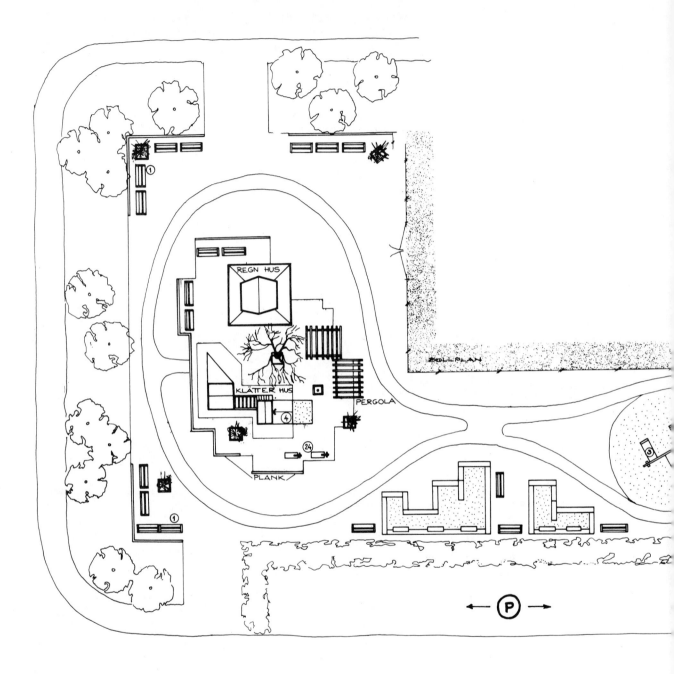

REGN HUS

KLÄTTER HUS

PERGOLA

PLANK

BOLLPLAN

SKALA 1:100

M 0   5

Stamgårdsparken
Since the playground is surrounded by busy streets parents must accompany their children here. This park is therefore unusually well visited by adults. Do traffic-free areas all too easily become adult-free areas?

Stamgårdsparken

A playground with poor physical attributes but which is nevertheless well planned, with a diversified social life, is Stamgårdsparken in Sundbyberg. The playground, which has recently been equipped with a large combination apparatus and many planks and fences creating enclosed spaces, has the character of a neighborhood park and is unsupervised. There are many adult visitors of all types, including workers on their lunch break, old men and other adults without children.

The playground as a whole feels spacious. All the equipment is easy to reach and there are benches all over. Considering the limited surface, the chances for variety are relatively great. Children can swing, climb, build in the sand, play ball. What is lacking is a more varied ground surface, especially something soft like grass.

Mothers and others looking after children have a lively relationship with each other. They seem to know each other and the playground seems to serve as a meeting place. Grown-ups take an active part in the children's play, and do not seem bored by being there. People do not distinguish so sharply between their own and others' children when it comes to giving help. There is in general a good feeling both among the adults and between children and adults.

The children get along well with each other. Most know each other, and they feel they "belong." Conflicts are very rare, most involve trivialities and are resolved quickly. The children talk quite a lot while they play. Young children (3 - 4 -year-olds) are accepted by the older children, who let them join in and help them when they need it. This has been observed among the boys, who are in the majority.

Judging from our observations, the rain shelter which is provided has a considerable effect on the number of visitors when the weather is grey. A cloudburst can be a very exciting experience. During a preliminary visit to the playground in the spring of 1974, a sudden cloudburst occurred. All the children, about ten of them between the ages of 3 and 11, together with the mothers present, rushed into the shelter, which is provided with a climbing net. The younger children and mothers sat on the benches. The bigger children climbed up the net to the little loft. The rain poured down in sheets from the edge of the roof. The children touched the falling water, listened to the sounds. The bigger children got very excited and shouted up to the heavens: "Listen, God, stop peeing!" Some of the children ran out into the rain and back again, soaking wet. When the rain stopped, everyone went out and splashed in the puddles and then returned to their play.

This playground is a fine example of how it is possible to provide cozy spaces and variety even when the starting-point is a flat surface in the middle of the city.

• *The many pleasant places to sit, enclosed by brightly-colored fences, are an obvious asset. A bench in the sand-pit increases the chances for close contact between children and grown-ups.*

• *The screens and playhouses divide up the space into passages and rooms and increases the opportunites to play peek-a-boo and hide-and-seek and to be together in small groups without being disturbed.*

12

How Supervised Playgrounds Are Used

In turning now to a description of supervised playgrounds, we begin with "Fisksätra" and "Orminge" in Nacka, then go on to discuss the play park in Hallonbergen, which has already been mentioned in the previous chapter, as well as "Nyby" which is located on Uppsalaslatten and "Upplands-Väsby" which in in the Norra Berget section of Upplands-Väsby.

We shall begin, as we did in the chapter on unsupervised playgrounds, by taking a look at what percentage of their time at the playground the observed children spent using fixed equipment as opposed to various playground surfaces.

Table 12-1 Percentage of time, on the average, that the children observed spent on fixed equipment and on ground surfaces at **supervised** playgrounds.

Name of the play-ground	On surfaces	On swings and in sand.	On other fixed equip-ment	Total
Fisksatra	69	10	21	100
Orminge	38×	18	44	100
Hallonbergen	59	18	23	100
Nyby	50	33	17	100
Upplands-Väsby	76	5	19	100

× = the larger grass and asphalt surfaces were not included in the observation area.

As we see here, children at supervised playgrounds have, with one exception, used the surfaces most: about 50 - 70% of the time spent at the playground. The low figure for Orminge has its explanation in the fact that the playground is so situated that the large open grass surfaces as well as certain asphalt surfaces lie outside the park itself and therefore have not been observed (a situation similar to the case of Sandvik). The low percentage of time that swings and sand were in use at Fisksatra is due to the fact that the sand-pits lie inside the enclosed area for small children, which was not observed. As Appendix 2 clearly shows, however, the children often played in the sand around the swings. The figures from Orminge reveal that the swings there are used very little, while other equipment is used much more than usual. In other play parks, the total time spent on ground surfaces, swings and in sand-pits accounted for 75 - 85% of the time that children were at the park. The figures, in other words, are about the same as for unsupervised playgrounds. Nevertheless, it seems that the surfaces at supervised playgrounds are used somewhat more, and that the swings at most supervised playgounds have a **low** rate of use.

We see that surfaces such as asphalt, grass and natural terrain get a great deal of use in all play parks, which indicates that playing with bikes and carts, hopscotch, twist, jump rope, roller skating, land hockey, high-jump,

Building something offers many opportunities to proceed by trial and error, learn from each other and work together. To be able to exert an influence, to decide yourself what to make, and to see the finished results is very satisfying. (carpentry corner, Orminge)

The contact city children have with animals is often slight and fleeting. It is very good that the 4H Club (Hand, Health, Head, Heart) works to give children the chance, under expert guidance, to take care of animals, feed them, and keep them clean—not only to pet them.

soccer, "rounds" (a game played in Sweden that bears a distant resemblance to baseball), boccie, tennis and badminton are all very common. Since different games require different surfaces, it is very important that both hard surfaces and soft surfaces such as grass and sand are available. The extent to which these surfaces are used shifts with the season. An example from Draken playground on Soder in Stockholm shows how a hard surface lends itself to various games. For a long time the only asphalt surface available at this playground was a path leading to the various entrances. In front of the entrance to the play park's indoor premises, the path widened somewhat and this little asphalt spot was always full of children roller-skating, playing land hockey or jumping rope, while the large gravel field nearby stood largely deserted.

Grass is an important foundation especially in the summer time for high-jumping and different ball games, and also for lying in the sun, being together, standing on one's head, wrestling, playing with animals and perhaps having a picnic.

That a natural area can be used in many ways and lead to rich experiences is obvious from what happened one day at Orminge play park in Nacka. Two boys rambled through the woods and, finding some string and boards, tried to build a hut against a rock. When they failed, they continued on and wound up in a natural "room" surrounded by rocks and small birches.

Water is an essential element at every playground. A complicated, expensive installation is not necessary. An ordinary pump works just fine.

Here they settled down for a long while, sat and smiled, talked and sang, almost hidden from the world around them. Carpentry, care of animals, and water play, when they are available, are all very popular. The fixed equipment used most is the same as at unsupervised playgrounds: sand-pits, slides and large combination climbing frames. Swings, on the other hand, were used very little at several of the supervised playgrounds we studied. Children have perhaps had their fill of swinging at their own local playgrounds.

Grown-ups are central figures for the child

We have already stated that access to play leaders can make the difference between night and day when it comes to how a playground functions. We have noticed, however, that some play parks function better than others, depending on how they are planned and where they are located.

The staff at a play park has, or should have, a double function. On the one hand, they should provide children with play materials and stimulate their play, and on the other they should serve as a sort of contact-point, a connecting link among the adults in the area and between adults and children. This latter function is by no means the least important, especially in suburbs where everyone is "new." We have seen examples both of how the staff can be helped and how it can be thwarted in its effort to manage this double role by the way the physical environment has been planned. In Fisksätra we have a clear example of an unsatisfactory solution.

Fisksätra
Design of the playground

The playground is a continuation and termination of the local playgrounds located all along Fisksätra Avenue. The play parks's indoor facilities are on the ground floor of the last apartment building. Apparently this playground was conceived of as a supplement and an alternative to playing in one's "own" yard. The park includes a fireplace, carpentry corner, aerial ropeway, cycle pit (velodrome), water-play installation and big slides. In addition the play park makes available loose materials such as a high-jump frame, different kinds of ball game equipment, excavators and other toys for use in the sand. There is also a chance for children to stay indoors and play board games, paint, look at films and take part in other special activities arranged from time to time. The play park premises have also been made available to pensioners' groups. At the request of the personnel and some of the parents, there is a supervised play group for young children several mornings a week. The personnel have, on their own initiative, also provided a chance for children to do some gardening.

This playground lies exposed to the wind blowing in from the nearby water. The wind shelters are not enough to provide a pleasant miniclimate.

Impression of monotony

Despite the fact that the park contains all these varied play possibilities, it gives the impression of being a repetition of the arrangement of equipment found at the local playgrounds in the area. A number of kinds of equipment fall into this category, including tractor-tire swing, ordinary swings, slides and small playhouses with roofs. Such equipment, moreover, recurs twice in this playground. The impression of repetition and monotony is further strengthened by the fact that there are rain-wind shelters for adults at three different places at the playground and also at regular intervals along Fisksätra Avenue. All in all, the playground feels dreary. It is spread out and lacks any real center.

Exposed to wind and weather

During our autumn observation period the weather was cold, windy and rainy. The weather was just as cold and bad at the beginning of the spring observation period but in the middle of May and the beginning of June it turned very warm. The playground is extremely vulnerable to wind and weather. Cold winds blow off the water nearby. The buildings and the little bit of woods that remain give no protection.

Not particularly well-used

Despite the shelters, the playground was little used in cold and nasty weather and the play areas were at such times often entirely deserted. On warm days, however, the number of visitors increased considerably. It is the grass and the water in particular that are inviting then.

When the weather was nice, mothers and others with children to look after came to the park, and also day-care center groups. We have only seen children from the day-care center close by, however, none from further away. Those who come generally stay a rather short time, a half-hour or forty-five minutes at the most. It often happens that mothers and their children stop at the park on their way somewhere else. The children go down the slide, swing, or climb up in the tower. Then they continue on their way. In the afternoon the park has more visitors. It is the ball fields that are most used then, regardless of weather. Also movable equipment, especially the high-jump, are popular, as well as the carpentry corner when it is open. On warm days the stream, pond and showers, together with the grass, are used, while the rest of the playground stands empty. Children riding bikes also visit. They often stay only to take a swing around the bicycle pit and ride awhile on the large asphalt surfaces.

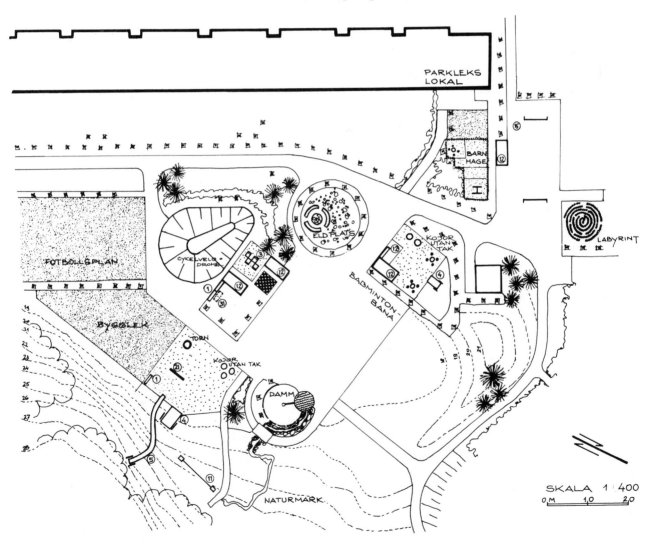

A lot of running back and forth for the staff

The indoor facility at a play park is a very important place. In order for the relationship between the play leaders and those using the park to work well, it is essential that it be close to the outdoor areas. Some children and mothers who visit this park go directly into the play park room. They stay there without using the outdoor facilities at all, except perhaps the play enclosure for small children right in front. The indoor space is situated too far away from the rest of the playground. If someone wants to fetch some loose play materials it is not such a short distance to go. This may be one of reasons why there is usually so little loose material belonging to the play park out on the playground. The personnel are seldom out either. They are too few in number, and it is too far to run back if the telephone rings or there is someone inside looking for them. Those working here experience this as a real conflict. Moreover, the location of the indoor facility has turned out to be a nuisance for the residents who have an entry and a little bit of yard right next to the play park. They have complained of being disturbed by the noise and the running in and out.

All this goes to prove that at the very least there should be a supplementary house with a supply of loose materials and perhaps a nice enclosed veranda to entice more mothers out in bad weather. It is a well-known fact (?!) that it is not children who get cold and want to go home but grownups. Also some such facility would give the park a natural center, and the present space could be used for other sorts of indoor activities.

An even worse location for play park premises is to be found at the play park Haren on Söder in Stockholm. There, it is necessary to go down some steps and around the building to reach the place. This arrangment is compensated for to some extent by the fact that there is a storage hut for loose materials on the playground itself. But it is far preferable if the play park house serves as a real center for both children and adults, as it does at the play park in Orminge.

Children spoil things, they are in the way, they cause trouble . . . When are we going to begin to change our attitudes and start taking children into account? (One of a series of posters on the preschool prepared by the Play Council)

Orminge

The play park in Orminge came into existence because of action taken by the residents themselves, who succeeded in getting a large park built and play leaders employed instead of settling for a few unsupervised small playgrounds, as had originally been planned.

Design of the playground

The park consists largely of natural terrain and is situated on a wooded, hilly site. The park itself rises like a little island above the houses and lawns near by. For this reason the park feels naturally set apart, even though it is not enclosed except around the carpentry area.

The play park house is a long, narrow, wooden structure painted yellow, with a veranda. In front of the veranda is the park's only asphalt surface, which is small, a sand-pit partly roofed over, and some permanent benches and tables. On a grassy hill in the woods there is a small, narrow slide fastened directly to the slope. A fenced-area with some swings is located at the edge of the woods near the hill. Below this, also at the edge of the woods, is a train, a house shaped like a mushroom, an indian tent, a wall for playing ball and climbing, a slate board and a wooden snail. Further off in the woods is an aerial ropeway and an "adventure park" which includes

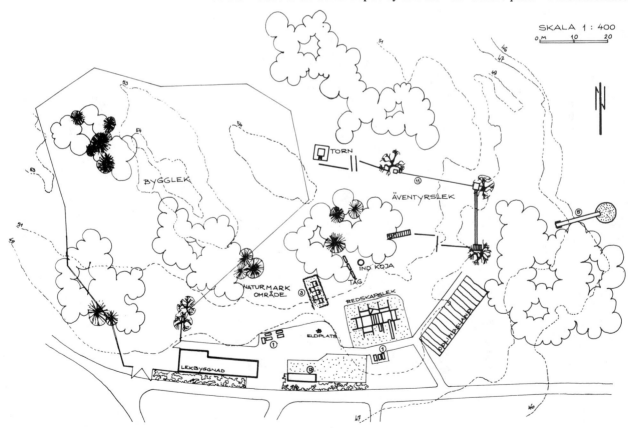

a tower with a small slide, logs for balancing, a place to crawl through, netting, ropes and poles. In front of the wooded hill, the park opens up on an area of sand and gravel where a large combination type of play equipment with a high, wide slide and a hammock has been situated. Beyond this is an enclosed area for gardening.

The carpentry area lies entirely in the woods. One enters it by way of a gate or through the play park house.

Shelter from wind and rain

The weather in the autumn was mostly cold and wet, and in the spring predominantly warm and sunny. Shelter from sun and rain is provided by the play park house veranda and, for children, under the roof which covers part of the sand-pit. The whole park is well protected from wind due to the many trees and the lack of large open areas.

How the play equipment and surfaces were used

The playground is fairly large and feels spacious because of the different

The woods provide pleasant shelter against wind and bad weather.

• *Hills and woods form natural boundaries and spaces which are nice to have when building.*

• *At this park children can play on many different kinds of surfaces: gravel, grass, rock, clay and asphalt.*

levels and because all the trees divide it up into a number of spaces which can be used separately. The presence of these smaller areas, each with its particular activity, such as gardening or carpentry, distinct character, and equipment suited to different age groups gives the park the feeling of being full of variety and chances for doing things.

One of the sub-areas, which feels like the park's center, is a rectangular asphalt surface bounded by the play park house, a sand-pit and a wooded hillside. The setting gives one the feeling of being in a "room" at the same time that it in no way feels closed in, since one can see out over the large grass lawn beyond the playground. This asphalt area continues as a path which ends outside the boundaries of the park. During the warm months of the year, it is this area that is most used by mothers and younger children. One reason for this is that it is sunny and calm here, there are lounge chairs available, and it is possible to buy coffee, juice and hot dogs. The mothers can talk together and still keep an eye on their children playing in the sand-pit or riding bikes on the asphalt. Bikes and carts are furnished by the park, and there are enough of these available, so that competition over them seldom occurs.

The mood between children and grown-ups and among the grown-ups themselves seems relaxed and friendly. Personnel do not arrange activities but are always there to take out things to play with, help out, or play games with the children when asked. The fact that grown-ups can buy a cup of coffee in the play park house has surely contributed to the good contact between parents and personnel. Parents seem to talk mostly with those they already know, but the get-togethers arranged in the winter, where one can paint, do textile printing, or model with clay may lead gradually to new friendships being formed.

Helping out with something "real" appeals to most children.

At larger parks where children come on outings now and then, the fixed equipment is not "used up" as fast as it usually is at a local park or preschool yard.

As in most parks, there are no special activities intended for grown-ups or for children and grown-ups together. The ping-pong table may be an exception; sometimes we saw adults playing there with each other or with children. Another exception may be gardening and farming. Planting, watering, pulling weeds and harvesting can be fun for both children and grown-ups.

The playground normally has a lot of visitors, which is probably due both to the appealing equipment and to the fact that it is a pleasant place for grown-ups.

At the local playgrounds in the area there is some fixed play equipment, but a large combination climbing frame, aerial ropeway and carpentry corner are found only at the play park and presumably this has much to do with its drawing power. Many preschool groups come on outings to the park, and it is above all the equipment just named which the children all run to. Their need to climb, jump and "let themselves go" is satisfied above all on the large combination climbing frame. The hammock in particular, and also the large slide, are very appealing. When preschool groups have visited the playground, the equipment has been invaded by as many as 40 children at one time, who go down the slide, jump into the hammock or play tag on the scaffolding. The equipment is challenging for children up to twelve, but even children under five manage to climb up to the slide and think it is fun and exciting to jump into the hammock. The younger children draw back quickly, however, when a group of older children appears on the scene, since these children often play very energetically and dominate the equipment. In order for such large combination equipment to be available for

• *Children like to wait for the wind to blow up the hammock like a bubble, then in they jump!*

• *Many playgrounds have a ping-pong table. Why is it used so little?*

younger children, there must only be a few children using it at one time. On several occasions it has happened that mothers have stopped their children from playing there when they felt it was dangerous. According to the personnel, there has never been an accident. The slide is quite high for younger children and it is therefore good that the park also has a small slide directly fastened to a grassy slope. Even two-year olds can climb up this hill and slide down.

The aerial ropeway is situated in the same part of the park as the large combination climbing frame, and one often sees children rush first to the large slide and then to the ropeway. The ropeway functions well for children from three to twelve. It offers the experience of dizzying speed, and can be used for rule games and different kinds of acrobatic feats. It encourages children to play together but can also be used by one child alone. Grownups can become involved in a natural way by helping the smaller children to get up.

The carpentry corner is on a wooded hillside, which makes it tempting to build little shacks, and it is large enough that each child or group of children can find their own spot for building. This area is used mostly by school children. Boys and girls 7 - 12 come in the afternoon and sometimes during their lunch recess. This activity is best suited for children of this age, but

The aerial ropeway encourages working and playing together.

children from about four on can enjoy building things as long as there is some grown-up present. Young children are of course unable to plan and think through how to go about building a shack, nor do they have the physical qualifications to manage the work themselves. Still, they are eager to join in and help others and seem to be stimulated by watching older children and play leaders at work. It is important to have a competent, experienced person as supervisor to make sure that the shacks are safely built and to serve as model, advisor and source of information.

Several children often worked together to build a house, but no large collective construction was undertaken. What was most important seemed to be the building activity itself. We never saw any further development, as for example a child "living" in the house he had made. One reason for this may be the scarcity of boxes, old wheels, bits of fabric and other "junk" which could be used in symbolic play.

In another part of the woods there is an "adventure park." To be able to grasp the relationship among the various pieces of equipment here and to realize that everything functions as a connected system, children need to be seven or older. Younger children can, with the help of adult supervision, use certain parts of the set-up, such as the crawl-through tunnel or the slide at the tower. This adventure park does not seem to appeal to children to any great extent, perhaps because it is situated a little out of the way. How

Here, starting from the natural setting itself, the opportunites for climbing have been extended.

This slide was left loose at the playground for several weeks. The children carried it around. Sometimes they pretended it was a boat. Here they have connected it to the train. Another time it was set up against a fence. Finally, the slide was mounted on a grassy slope where it is an excellent complement to a large, wide slide. Even the youngest children can manage to use this slide.

pieces of equipment are grouped in relation to each other has an important impact on how play develops. In Orminge there is a train, a mushroom-house, an indian tent and a wooden snail placed together on a wooded hillside. The children seem to regard these objects as a unit and play, for example, that they live in the indian tent, buy tickets in the mushroom-house and ride the train to work.

Swings are used much less here than at other parks, perhaps because there are other things that are more appealing and also because the swings are in a somewhat shady and inconvenient place up in the woods. Small children cannot go there alone but are dependent on the initiative of grown-ups, who in turn seem to find it more pleasant to sit in the asphalt area at the sand-pit. At other playgrounds it is usual to see older children using the swings for sitting and talking together but at Orminge the hammock on the climbing frame seems to fill this function. The sand-pit is used a great deal, mostly by preschool children. Its central location in an area where mothers enjoy sitting and the availability of loose equipment like excavators undoubtedly contribute to its popularity.

Hallonbergen

It has already been noted that the relationship between indoor and out-door facilities at supervised playgrounds varies considerably from place to place and has an important bearing on how the playground functions as a whole. There are many examples where the somewhat inconvenient location of the indoor premises has been compensated for by some sort of storage shed on the playground itself. This solution has worked very well at the play park in Hallonbergen, where the indoor facilities are on the ground floor of an apartment building. We have previously mentioned that this playground works well because it has a center **and** many separated areas where children can play undisturbed.

Another thing that is attractive about Hallonbergen's play park is the wealth of loose materials available, especially cars, carts, and bicycles. There are also doll buggies, blankets, and dolls. Inside the playhouse there is doll furniture. The wish for construction materials has proved to be so great that an additional chest filled with building blocks was added in the spring. In the sand-pit are three excavators and a large number of carts, shovels of different sizes, pails, and molds, unfortunately all of plastic. There are also lots of balls and games.

Our impression is that the staff are very eager to provide the children with materials; they take out things to play with even in rain and bad weather, which stimulates developing play. They also put out buckets of water by the sand-pit for playing in the sand and watering the flowers. Moreover, they put a lot of effort into distributing the materials fairly and seeing to it that nothing gets lost.

We have observed other play parks where the personnel are outdoors ex-tremely little. This usually happens because the park is under-staffed. The available play leaders simply cannot manage to "keep watch" indoors and at the same time be outdoors. Sometimes, however, it has seemed to us that it is the content of the activity itself that causes the problem. There is not anything meaningful for an adult - play leader or parent - to do outdoors if his own appetite for play is exhausted. Why can it not be the common responsibility of the personnel and the visitors to look after things? Why are play leaders **only** trained to take care of children? It is interested, involved, active adults that children need to meet at the playground.

PARK-
LEKS
LOKAL

PORT

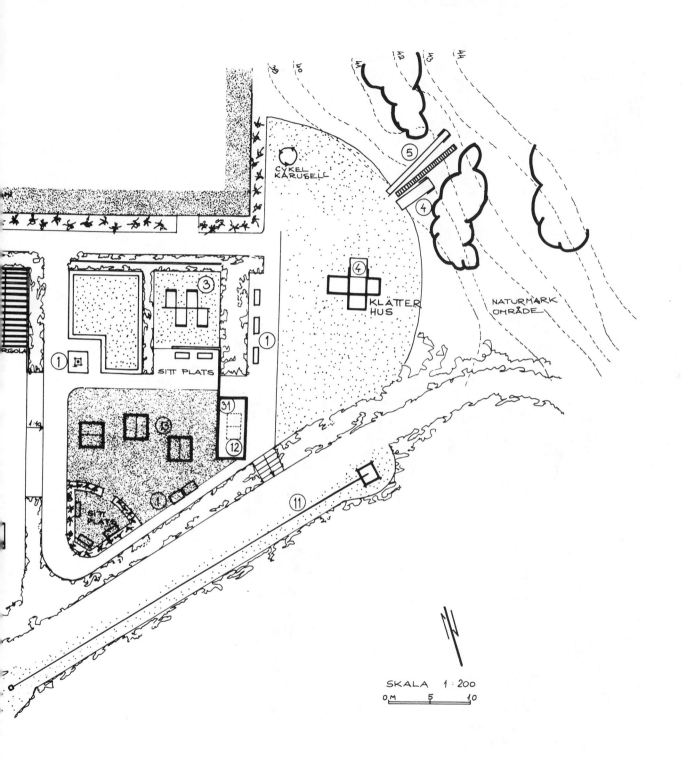

CYKEL
KARUSELL

⑤

④

KLÄTTER
HUS

NATURMARK
OMRÅDE

③

①

① ▣

SITT PLATS

㉛

⑫

①

SITT
PLATS

⑪

SKALA   1 : 200

0M   5   10

- *Excavators appeal to children from an early age. It is interesting to figure out how they work. Several children often play together and help each other load sand.*

- *Wagons and carts, simply designed with not too many details, appeal to childrens imagination.*

- *A chest of building blocks has much to offer. Here the blocks are bars of gold and the boards are machine-guns. The game is to defend the "treasure."*

- *To build a tiny dark room and then creep in is exciting and cozy.*

Originally the idea was that this playground would extend from the rocky hill down into the valley. The proposal was cut back a good deal and the final result was a flat, squeezed-in play area which, despite everything, functions well.

The play park in Orminge, because of its setting and its location in the area, offers very good opportunities for play. Unfortunately, we found conditions to be otherwise at the park in Nyby.

Nyby

The residential area

The playground is situated between a recently built single-family area and a new apartment-building complex. The housing has been built by Svenska Riksbyggen and planned for about 5000 residents. People have moved in gradually over the past several years. By the summer of 1975 all the apartments, which are cooperatively owned, were occupied. There are both high (five-story) and lower (two and three-story) buildings. The area includes an extensive service center with post office, shops, facilities for pensioners, a medical office, school and day-care center. The local playgrounds in the apartment building complex are equipped with swings, sand-pits, climbing apparatus, peak-houses and backboards.

Design of the playground

The playground is situated on a large grass-covered site between the two residential areas. It is flat except for some artificial mounds. The park building is in the center and around it are grouped various play areas. Behind it is a place for small children to play, in front a swimming pool and expansive lawn. To one side is a large sand area with a lot of fixed equipment and on the other side about 50 meters away a carpentry area. In the park building itself children have a chance to listen to a tape recorder, play ping-pong or simply withdraw into a cozy corner. This happens mostly when the weather is bad. In addition, the staff arranges certain indoor activities from time to time, such as movies. Loose equipment includes stilts, hockey clubs, equipment for various kinds of ball games, excavators, carts and a high-jump.

Children can borrow these things in the afternoon when a play leader is there. The large grass area is well-suited for various games, such as boccie. In addition, there is a gravel field and a tennis court, but these are used rather little. The drained pool was used for playing land hockey since the playground contains only a small asphalt surface.

Materials for construction such as hammers, nails, and helmets are also available when someone on the staff is present. The carpentry area is enclosed by grassy banks but is open so that children can go there and play whenever they want.

A line-up of play equipment for somewhat older children was planned as a complement to these other activities. In a rectangular sand-pit are three play-houses, a combination frame with ropes, rope ladder and netting, a big playhouse, swings and balance beams.

There are benches around the park house, at the pool and at the equipment line-up. No shelter exists except for the closed-in veranda at the park house.

No protection from wind

The area is flat and there are no full-grown trees or bushes, so there is no place that is protected from the wind. Nor is the playground divided into

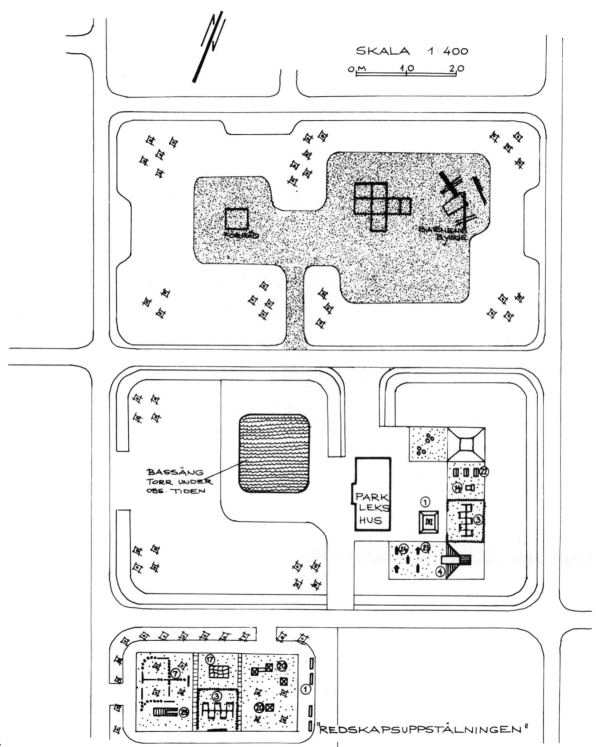

SKALA 1:400

0M   1,0   2,0

ISKRÅD

SVACKAND RYGGE

BASSÄNG
TORR UNDER
OBS. TIDEN

PARK
LEKS
HUS

①

"REDSKAPSUPPSTÄLNINGEN"

Nyby.

sub-areas in any way, so that it feels open and exposed, without any coziness. The constant draught intensifies this impression.

The place that is sunniest and least windy is next to the wall of the park building on the side facing the pool, and on the veranda. This, however, is not of much use to parents with small children, since the play area for them is on the other side of the house. One could wish for a screened, sheltered corner in a sunny part of the small children's enclosure, and some moveable sun-chairs or benches which could be put where it is nicest to sit depending on the sun and wind, would also be welcome. In addition, a rain shelter is much needed.

The play area for small children is very exposed to the wind and does not contain much to discover or explore.

How play equipment and surfaces were used

Children do not need to cross any streets in order to get to the playground from the surrounding residential neighborhood. Older children can therefore go to the park themselves, but for children under five or so the distance from home is too great to go alone.

The playground occupies a large area. There are many different places to play and many different things to do. Nevertheless it can feel like there is not enough room, since the children tend to congregate in certain places. The older children keep to the places where personnel are to be found, at the park house or carpentry area, and the small children stay in the area intended especially for them.

The playground has many sorts of equipment and it is probably the reason why parents with young children are attracted here. They stay mostly in the enclosed area and gently see to it that their children stay there also. The children often bring buckets and shovels with them and the sand is in constant use for baking cakes and digging. The swings and rocking horses are also used.

The plastic module was used for climbing on and crawling through, and also inspired make-believe play, serving as a car or engine. The three small playhouses did not stimulate fantasy play. The younger children explored them, touched the roof and floor, poured sand into them and sometimes sought protection there when it was windy.

Of the loose equipment, the excavators were most popular, which sometimes caused problems. Other things like carts were also available, however, which encouraged constructive solutions to conflicts, since one child could load the sand and another take it away. Several times this led to group play among children who did not previously know each other.

The equipment set-up for the somewhat older children was visited now and then by adults with small children and by older children. But a common sight in the afternoon was the crowd of children at the carpentry corner and around the park house, while this equipment stood completely empty. Even though this area is full of equipment it feels barren somehow since it is in no way divided into smaller areas. Because so few used this equipment, it was here that children could withdraw and play undisturbed. Of the equipment here, the blue playhouse was used most, by little children to play peek-a-boo and by older children for climbing and rule games. One time several boys found some sheets of cardboard and they laid them out and played "don't-touch-the-sand", making use of the entire area. It was fairly common for children to try out briefly the various pieces of equipment and then leave this part of the park.

Among older children, land hockey, which was played in the swimming pool, was a very popular pastime. High-jumping was also popular with children seven years' old and over.

Sometimes the staff initiated different types of bowling games on the open grassy area. According to them, "rounds" was also played there in the evening. The carpentry area is surrounded by grassy banks which make this the coziest and most sheltered part of the entire playground. It was not an uncommon sight to see 20 or 30 children in full swing there. Building was enjoyed not only by school children, but by younger children as well. Instead of using hammer and nails, they took loose boards and placed them against some structure already built, fantasized about what they would make and played "workmen." The children often played on a climbing frame they had built themselves. This "homemade" arrangement had a slide that was high and exciting, and there were many nooks and corners to creep into. Children built no small shacks of their own; the flat gravel surface did not encourage this. Instead they workded on large joint projects. During our observation time there were considerably more boys than girls using the carpentry corner.

• *Plastic play equipment, is it beautiful or ugly? Many plastic playthings cannot tolerate the winter cold and crack.*

• *The equipment "line-up" is a place to go if you want to be left alone. These houses have sometimes been used for playing tag by bigger children and for hide-and-seek and peek-a-boo by small children and grown-ups together.*

• *Here is an original way to use a fence. Loose materials which can be used to rebuild and change things are eagerly "sucked up" at playgrounds. Movable ladders would be an excellent complement in many play areas.*

Number of visitors very
dependent on the weather

In the morning the playground was visited by children up to five, accompanied by their mothers or some other grown-up. The number of children depended very much on the weather. When it was windy or rainy, or even if it was just grey and cloudy, the playground was normally deserted. In the afternoon the number of children present also varied depending on the weather, but since some indoor activities were available then, there were always at least some children there. One group of children about ten years' old always came and seemed to feel at home at the playground. They knew the personnel and used the carpentry area a great deal. On the final days of our spring observation period, the playground was also visited by some teenagers (who had finished with school for the year). Presumably the number of visitors to the playground will increase in the coming years as the children in the neighborhood grow older and get to know each other.

Helping to do something "real"

Contacts among adults at this playground can be described as neutral. A few mothers of young children talked together, but most had no contact at all with each other. The size of the staff varied; most often, there were only two play leaders, which meant that their chances to arrange different types of activities were very limited. They saw to it that loose materials such as carts and excavators were taken out, sometimes participated in games, and helped with the carpentry corner. When building activity was in full swing, two leaders were needed to supervise and make sure that nothing dangerous happened. The children's need for contact with grown-ups was obvious. They often followed after the personnel and appreciated it when they were allowed to help do something "real." On one occasion, for example, cleaning up in the carpentry area engaged most of the children present.

Nyby is built on a level, windy site. Most of it is man-made and the planners have not succeeded in creating any great degree of variety and intimacy. The main meeting places are the park house and the carpentry corner. It is here that children find shelter from the wind, grown-ups, and loose materials. The array of fixed equipment is rarely used by anyone.

At Norra Berget in Upplands-Väsby the conditions are entirely different and the results more positive.

Upplands-Väsby

The playground Norra Berget in Upplands-Väsby was built with the aim of satisfying the leisure needs of both children and grown-ups. There is a water play area with canals, bridges, island and an outdoor shower, a meadow for animals with a pony, goats and rabbits, a place to buy coffee and juice at a low price, a grill, a barracuda-type tent where one can play tennis free, a lit-up track and a soccer field which can be frozen for skating in the winter. During the warm months musical programs and dances are arranged. To be sure, most of the grown-ups who come to the park during the day are young women - mothers, teachers, and others who care for children - but the chance to engage in various sports and go to dances and cultural events helps attract other people as well. On several occasions an "animal-day" has been organized, with exhibits, lectures and information so that children and grown-ups could learn together how to take care of pets like rabbits and fish. This is an excellent example of how it is possible to arrange activities that are of interest to both children and grown-ups.

Residential area

Upplands-Väsby a community north of Stockholm, is fairly spread out. There are both older and newer houses, some industry, as well as schools and the usual service facilities.

The play park is immediately adjacent to a nature area, Norra Berget. A relatively new shopping center with multi-story apartment buildings is not far away. The park often receives visitors from other areas as well as Upplands-Väsby.

Design of the playground

The playground itself is built up in successive levels against a rocky slope. It is surrounded by natural terrain on three sides. A large asphalt area with benches all around comprises the first "terrace." Here the play park house, which also serves as an after-school child center, is situated. The asphalt surface is used for various ball and other games. A steep paved hill with steps leads up to the next terrace, which contains a hilly asphalt surface with a water-play installation. This section of the playground is used a great deal even when the water is not turned on. A fort consisting of three wooden huts of various sizes, as well as some benches and tables, are also here. An asphalt slope with steps and a slide connects this level with the next, which is a large sand area with swings and equipment for climbing and balancing. An area for small children with a large playhouse lies off to one side. Finally, another asphalt slope with steps leads to the natural wooded area, where there is a large, long slide, suspension-bridge, aerial ropeway and three look-out towers. The large slide lies within the field of vision of a person entering the park and many children run immediately through the whole park to get to it.

Along one entire side of the park there is a meadow for goats and ponies and a little house for the children's own rabbits. Between this meadow and

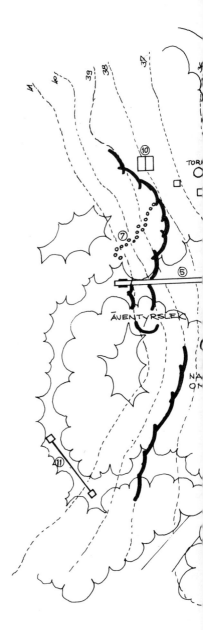

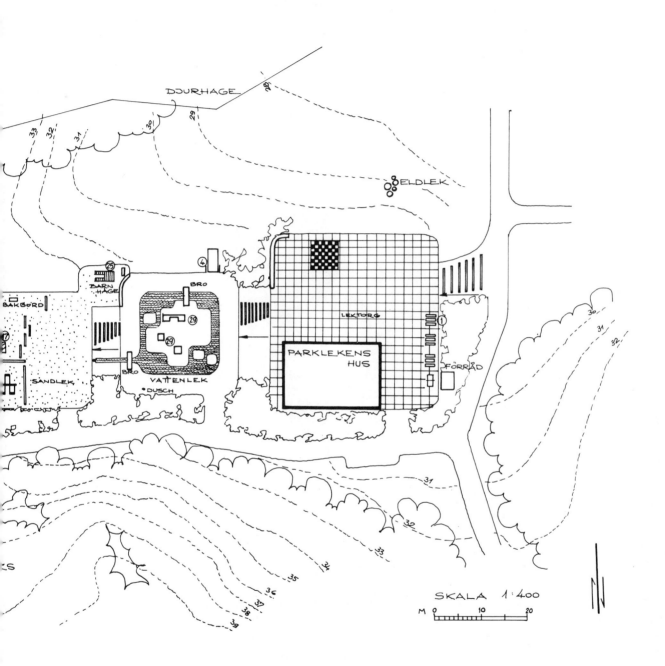

The ropeway is popular; it offers many chances for speed, imaginative play and cooperation. A ropeway without a tire-seat can be a death trap, however. Since the ropeway is a piece of equipment which is rather easily damaged and then becomes very dangerous, it should be possible to lock it when necessary.

A large, high, wide slide provides speed and excitement.

the rest of the playground is a rolling lawn. On the lower level there is a grill set into the grass. Loose equipment such as cars, wagons, clubs, balls and games are available and much used.

Inside the park building one can buy coffee, juice, sandwiches, rolls, ice cream, stewed fruit, etc, There are also newspapers, an aquarium, supplies for indoor play and a slide suspended from the ceiling with a thick mat under it, which is used a lot on cold and rainy days.

A lot to explore

When one stands down at the park house and looks up over the playground, it seems long and sprawling. This, together with the large paved surfaces, could easily give a cold and dreary impression, but such is not the case. Because of the surrounding natural area and the distinct levels or terraces, one experiences the site as a gentle swelling up to the wooded hills, and it is understandable that children race enthusiastically up the

It is interesting to find out what burns, how it smells, how to start a fire. And it builds confidence to know you can control fire.
Food cooked outdoors always tastes extra good!

slopes to explore the different levels. The strategic location of the large slide up on the rocky slope, together with the distinct levels, mean that the rest of the playground is explored "afterwards." Since each terrace, moreover, offers a particular kind of activity, the excitement of the playground's design and character is enhanced still further.

Despite the fact that the playground is located a little out of the way, it seems popular. It attracts children and grown-ups both, and groups of children often come here with their lunches and stay for some while. This is probably due to the fact that the playground includes activities for most age groups, that it possesses lovely surroundings and a good miniclimate, and that it is pleasant for adults to come and sit here. There is no car traffic, so even younger children can wander about on their own. What we have seen that can be dangerous are the steep asphalt slopes and the asphalt surface of the water-play area, which, during those times when the water is turned off, is used mostly for driving cars and carts around. In addition, high structures are standing on an asphalt foundation. If someone gets knocked down, falls or jumps from one of these he can get hurt rather badly, and we saw this happen several times.

Here the area's natural setting has been taken into consideration. Unfortunately even at this playground there is a "landscape" of static equipment and sand.

How the play equipment and surfaces were used

The playground is visited by children of all ages, from the youngest up to 13 - 14-year-olds. The youngest are of course accompanied by an adult. We saw mothers who were taking their turn on "playground duty" sitting with a cup of coffee and talking together while the children played in the sand or went down the slide next to the small children's play area.

The somewhat older children, 3 - 5 years' old, who were also usually accompanied by an adult or came as part of a day-care group, used the entire park to a large extent, even though most of their time was spent around the water-play area and the park house. Children 5 - 6 years' old normally used the whole playground. Larger groups most often visited the high slide, the animal meadow and the aerial ropeway. Making a great deal of noise, the children went down the slide as fast as possible or dared each other to pet and feed the animals.

Bigger children (7 - 10 years' old) played mostly around the park house or up in the woods, at least when the water-play installation was not working. They used the asphalt at the park house to play land hockey together with the staff. It was also this age group that made the most use of the loose equipment that was available.

When playing with water, children and grown-ups take part on the same terms. It is so-o-o-o nice to cool off. And it is fun to splash and make a lot of noise.

• *Many big-city children lack the chance for close contact with animals.*

• *If the rabbits are to have food, it must be grown. Farming involves many steps where children and grown-ups are needed to help out. Digging, watering, planting, pulling weeds.—These are activities where one works hard, gets exercise, cooperates, discusses, smells things, splashes with water, gets dirty, keeps busy. No one is ever finished learning. Children and grown-ups can share what they know and help each other, each one according to his ability.*

In general, one can say that the whole playground was used more or less evenly, except that the water-play area was overwhelmingly the most popular when it was in action. Then, **all** the children gathered there. Of the equipment at the park, the large slide and the loose equipment were most used by all age groups except the very youngest, who mostly played in the sand. The surfaces used most were the grass and asphalt, as well as the meadow where the animals are kept, while the large sand area with its climbing equipment was seldom used. It is a little surprising that the natural areas were not used more than they were. Nevertheless, we can see from the order of the items in Appendix 2 that they were used more than any fixed equipment except for the slides. Up in the woods we saw children playing such games as "war", hiding behind big rocks and using sticks for rifles.

Someone to take care of

The animal pasture with goats and pony is popular and well visited. All the children spend at least a little time with the animals when they come to the playground. A trained keeper has charge of them, so they get excellent care and the children also get sensible and satisfactory answers to their questions. Not only does contact with the animals provide a rich experience, both because of the feelings involved and what can be learned, but also we have noticed that a visit to the animals can promote contacts both among children and between children and grown-ups. Adults often find some excuse to start up a conversation, and young children feel more secure if there is some grown-up around when the pony comes galloping up to them! The rabbit hutch, where a number of children keep their own rabbits, seems to work well and large groups, mostly of girls, come to take care of and exercise their pets.

13
Play Equipment
in Its Setting

Placement

One of the most important factors influencing how much a piece of equipment is used has to do with whether it is situated centrally or not and whether adults can sit comfortably near by or take an active part in what is going on. The importance of these factors has been apparent again and again when we have analyzed our observations. It appears that each playground has some gathering place; it may be the swings, the bars, a large jungle gym, an asphalt surface where many pass by, or the play park house or storage shed. The equipment or area which takes on this function of gathering place naturally has a high frequency of use. At one playground such equipment as swings, bars, sand-pit or climbing frame can be extremely popular and even indispensable while at another playground the identical equipment may stand completely idle. We can state for example that swings, which are usually greatly appreciated by children, were hardly used at all at the playground in Orminge due to their somewhat inconvenient location and the stiff competition from other exciting facilities, while the sand-pit with its central and sheltered location was used very much. At the play park Haren on Söder in Stockholm the bar was used very often, as it was at **one** other playground studied, while at the majority of playgrounds it was mostly ignored because it was not in a central location, and also perhaps because other equipment satisfied the need for this type of exercise instead, making the bar superfluous. While some equipment is particularly "sensitive" when it comes to the relationship between location and

The heart of the play park. (Orminge)

frequency of use, there is a tendency for **all** equipment to show some variation in use due to placement - even such popular and versatile equipment as chests of building blocks and aerial ropeways.

Certain equipment, then, functions better if centrally placed so that, in addition to its intrinsic value, it can also serve as a meeting place for children. Other types of equipment, however, function better if put in a secluded, undisturbed part of the playground, where the children have a chance to develop their play in peace and quiet. This applies to huts and play-houses in particular, to store-fronts and also to sand-pits and building blocks. Another decisive factor, of course, in promoting use of such equipment is access to cloths to hang up, dishes and buckets to collect stones, cones and leaves in, and dress-up clothes. Because such supplementary loose materials have often been lacking at the playgrounds studied, playhouses have not at all served their intended function.

An illuminating example of how the total layout of the site influences the use of play equipment was observed at Hallonbergen, where the far end of the playground was recently provided with benches. Before the benches were put there, the equipment in that part of the playground - a combination climbing frame with slide, two slides bedded in the rocky slope, and a bicycle carousel - were used infrequently. After the benches were added, adults enjoyed sitting in this area and the equipment was used more often.

A well-planned setting, we are convinced, can support and improve the value of play equipment and even in many respects compensate for the fact that some of the equipment does not function as hoped. But more than that, a carefully thought-out plan for the playground site as a whole can offer both children and grown-ups experiences of a different dimension than play equipment alone can provide.

These were used more often when benches were set out near by.

Grouping of equipment

At many playgrounds equipment stands stiffly and monotonously arrayed in rows. Often, unfortunately, several pieces of equipment with much the same function are put next to each other. We have concluded from our observations that when several facilities with the same basic function - such as a climbing frame and a look-out platform - stand close together, **each one** of them is used extremely sporadically. On the other hand, if a playground has only **one** object for climbing and getting a view, it is used much more often than several similar objects taken together and in a much more flexible way. This can be compared to the experience many parents have of cleaning out their child's toy chest only to discover that the child plays much more with his toys afterwards, when he has fewer things to confuse him. Then the challenge lies in doing something with the toys left! This same principle of "too much of a good thing" applies to playground equipment. The landscapes of equipment found at several playgrounds we have visited are undoubtedly arranged as they are for reasons of economy. It is cheaper to make **one** large sand area than several. But this is false economy. The result, ironically, is to create a place where a child goes if he wants to be alone for a bit, **not** where he goes if he wants to play. Surely there must a better and cheaper way to arrange for a little privacy! Such accumulations of play equipment cannot be regarded as examples of good planning.

Play equipment has its greatest value when new, while a new tree is worth very little. The value of the tree grows as the tree itself grows, while the value of play equipment only declines.

Lillie

Arranging equipment in groups can, however, sometimes enhance the value of an individual piece of equipment, as an example from Orminge play park clearly illustrates. There a snail, a train and a mushroom-house have been grouped together on a wooded slope. This arrangement has proved stimulating for play. Other types of equipment suitable for such grouping include playhouses or combination structures that encourage make-believe games of the type that one person goes to visit another, as well as wilder rule games like tag. It is important to remember that a group need not consist of three identical houses; it can consist instead of an opening in a hedge, a stump or a rock supplemented with a playhouse. Or if the natural setting itself does not provide such opportunities, then complementary types of equipment can be arranged together, as in the Orminge example.

Spoiling the play surface

One often sees playground equipment arranged as a sequence of individual units forming what is referred to in Sweden as a "shipwreck." Many of us can remember those special days in the school gym when **all** the equipment was taken out at once! What a party! Manufacturers and planners seem to have a fond memory of these special moments and to wish to duplicate them at playgrounds, but what they forget is that much of the excitement of these occasions lay in the fact that they were something uncom-

Can it really be a contribution to the play environment to put several pieces of fixed equipment with the same function right next to each other?

This climbing frame is in no way special. But since there is a scarcity of fixed equipment at this playground, and since the children had access to ropes, large cloths and other loose materials, it was used considerably more—than usual.

mon, something new. Think if we had never done anything else in gym class but played on a shipwreck! How much fun would that have been? Only in exceptional cases have we seen children use these facilities as intended. It is often much too difficult for small children to grasp the total set-up, and when children are old enough to do so, then the individual pieces have long since become too easy for them and lost all interest. What is even more unfortunate, however, is that these collections of equipment take up a large part of the open space set aside for children and so do more to interfere with play than to promote it.

Coordination of equipment and setting

If the fixed play equipment is to form a meaningful unit together with the surroundings, then the equipment and the setting must mutually reinforce and enrich each other. A suspension-bridge has no meaningful function if it does not go over something. It does not necessarily have to cross a water-course, even if a creek naturally provides endless opportunities for experimentation and sensory experience. The bridge can pass over a bicycle or pedestrian path or stretch of sand on a lower level. It is very good also if the bridge can be used to get from one part of the playground to another.

A good example of how it is possible by means of proper planning to strengthen the function of both the setting and the equipment is to put a look-out tower on the highest point of the playground and thereby intensify the experience of height. Attaching a slide to an existing or man-made slope is also highly recommended. The chances for younger children to use the slide are thereby substantially increased, the danger of accidents diminishes, and children can run up and slide down at their own pace without being blocked or knocked down by others. But in planning such slide-slope arrangements, it must be remembered that a playground should function well year-round. It is therefore not desirable to ruin a hill used for sledding or skiing by filling it up with equipment, nor to put a metal slide on a hill facing south as it will get too hot in the summer.

If a playground borders on a wooded area, it can be advantageous to place some of the larger pieces of equipment, perhaps those not so suitable for small children, up in the woods. This encourages city children unaccustomed to such a setting to venture into the woods, perhaps to discover a pine cone or an ant. It is best if the playground does not have a very distinct boundary and if children can be allowed to go exploring without being dragged back into the play area proper all too soon by a grown-up!

Finally, what more splendid combination of equipment and setting exists than having a large tree with its delightful shade and glittering leaves enhance the pleasure of swinging? We all remember the wonderful sensation of leaning far back in a swing and peering up at the sky through the leaves or just managing to touch a branch with the tips of the toes!

14
Fixed Play Equipment Function and Safety

Fixed play equipment can be divided into two main groups according to function:

I.   Equipment or physical exercise

II.   Equipment for pretending, creating and constructing

These two main groups can in their turn be divided into sub-groups as follows:

I a. Equipment for exercise, simple function

   b. Equipment for exercise, in which movement is combined with the sensory experiences of speed, spinning, and dizziness.

   c. Equipment for exercise, combination type, in which movement is combined with one or more other functions such as sensory experience, symbolic play and rule games.

II a. Static representational equipment

   b. Room-creating equipment

   c. Construction materials

A comprehensive description of the function and frequency of use of the various types of play equipment observed in our study is to be found in appendix 3. Equipment with an extremely **low** frequency of use belongs primarily to groups I a and II a but also in some cases to groups I b and II b.

This appendix includes information about the way children of various ages have used the equipment, what loose materials have enriched play, and how the equipment should be situated to function at its best. In those cases where some type of fixed equipment proved to have no play value, we make brief suggestions about how it might be possible through well thought-out planning of the environment to increase the chances of its filling the intended function. This summary is accompanied by drawings of the different types of equipment that have been observed.

These static balance beams are not inspiring to play on. How could anyone imagine they would be? (Nyby)

Comments on the frequency of use of play equipment

The frequency of use of many types of fixed play equipment, as actually observed in our study, was in sharp contrast to what the descriptions in the catalogues of many play equipment manufacturers would lead one to believe. Nearly half of the equipment studied was used for only 0 - 2% of the time children played at a playground! Other equipment had an average rate of use of 3 -5 %, meaning that children spent 2 - 3 minutes of each hour using the facility in question. It is worth noting that even play equipment that was used comparatively often was not in use more than an average of 15 - 20 %of the total play time. And this was true despite the fact that the method we used involved observing a child from the time he **first** arrived at the playground, which if anything led to an overstatement of the frequency of use of fixed equipment since a child often "gets done with" such equipment first and then goes on to some other, more lasting type of play. It is above all swings at unsupervised playgrounds, slides bedded in a slope, combination equipment, playhouses where there is access to loose materials, and construction materials such as building blocks and sand which have the highest use on the average among children 1-10 years' old. In addition, several types of equipment that combine physical exercise with sensory experience have a relatively high rate of use among children of the age for which the equipment is intended, as for example rocking horses for small children and aerial ropeways and suspension-bridges for bigger children.

A climbing frame with lots of play opportunities. Everything is possible with the two climbing nets, tire ladder, ropes and climbing ladder. Generous size and high quality materials.

Children never get tired of climbing. They are always discovering new ways to master the equipment. The climbing wall gives many children a chance to climb at the same time. The climbing surface is soft and pleasant. There are also two attractive swings in the car tire and the rope ladder.

Future circus artists and sailors get their fill of practice in climbing.

Klängis has a generous climbing surface so many children can play together. The goal which everyone practices reaching is to be able to cross over from one side to the other.

Group I: Equipment for physical exercise

Equipment type I a

Equipment such as so-called "ship-wreck" systems, as well as balance beams, low jungle-gyms and equipment with only a climbing function (both of wood and steel) are used **infrequently** and most often for a **short** time only, about 2 minutes.

All these types of equipment have proved to have a **low** functional value. The reason for this is **not** that children have no need to climb, do acrobatic feats, or balance. Indeed, their need for these types of exercise is great. That this equipment is used so little and in such a limited way and only by certain age groups is probably due to its being so static and inflexible. If we want to construct good equipment and design a good play environment, we must understand clearly what needs the equipment and playground as a whole should satisfy and how children of different ages play. Children have a great need to **move**; they need equipment on which they can climb, creep, jump and romp about. But the equipment that exists today to satisfy this need mostly functions badly. The fact that nothing can be changed, that everything is so ready-made, causes children to lose all desire to climb. It is more exciting to go somewhere else. We must view physical exercise as one function among many which the playground should serve. If we separate the child's need for active exercise from his needs for social interaction and stimulation, then the child will not make use of the playground in the way intended. To avoid such mistakes, we must take into consideration a number of factors when we plan for children's physical exercise.

Equipment that has only a climbing function is quickly "used up." (Upplands-Väsby) The text in the picture is taken from a catalogue—

Antra is a whole little "department store" full of adventures for children. It always offers some new way to play. Children play together with others of various ages. They grow with Antra and never tire of it. The very youngest swing. The next stage is to climb up the rope ladder—then jump and swing. Those a little older climb higher. Go to the very top. Hang by the arms. And jump down. We make six variations so you can more easily include an Antra in your play environment.

The need to move finds an outlet in many ways other than climbing. Children tend to move about energetically in connection with all activities they engage in. Sailing a boat in a pond can be tremendously exciting and cause a child to dash from one side of the pond to the other and back again innumerable times. Running with a kite, riding a bike, pulling a friend in a wagon, heaving a bucket of sand up to the roof of a playhouse, lugging a board to a building site, pumping water, digging in a garden, raking leaves, being chased by a goat - all provide exercise and practice in gross muscular coordination.

Let us, therefore, avoid giving children static balance beams, obstacle courses, low walls, mazes and an abundance of climbing equipment. Let us instead satisfy their need to move about, balance, climb, and jump in a meaningful context.

If one starts with a broad view of children and their needs, then it is clear that functional and safety aspects hang together very closely. From this point of view it is entirely uninteresting to investigate how to make functional, inadequate, dull equipment safe. Such equipment is already "safe" since no one uses it! That such equipment as the "revolving barrel" is still available from certain manufacturers is an insult to children. That it is obviously dangerous (broken teeth) is basically irrelevent since its lack of any functional value whatever means that it should not exist at all where children play.

Aside from the fact that climbing equipment that serves only that purpose is unsuitable from a functional viewpoint, several sorts have proved dangerous, especially for small children. The parts of such equipment which we regard as particularly critical when it comes to safety are steps and ladders. We have observed again and again, and had it called to our attention

Backboards

Playing ball is enjoyed equally by boys and girls. Throughout the year except when there is snow on the ground the ball is a favorite plaything.

Having a blackboard at the playground helps give children a chance to play together and develop their ball sense. The walls come in modules which can be assembled in whatever lengths and with however many right angles you wish, providing the playground with a backboard that is much appreciated and a wind screen. A backboard with holes is fun for younger children and for the special ball games played by girls. A wall with goals marked on it is fine for children with dreams of playing soccer, handball or hockey.

by mothers as well, that a ladder formed from slanting strips of wood constitutes an unforeseeable risk for small children. The fact that the ladder is slanted makes it possible for very small children to climb up. From a functional viewpoint this is excellent since small children can gain an exhilarating feeling of height. But the long distance between the two sides of the ladder and between successive rungs makes it very easy for a small child to slip and damage a tooth.

Another safety problem associated with climbing devices is protruding edges where children can get their clothes caught or trip. Such equipment is now forbidden by law in Sweden. But it is the **foundation** on which climbing equipment stands that is most important of all for safety. We have seen many climbing frames placed on hard-packed gravel. It is also very common to have sand under such equipment, which means that small children are attracted to play there. In some playgrounds the entire sand area is furnished with equipment. This is both an obstacle to children's sand-building activities and a safety risk since children who fall or jump from a climbing frame can crash into a child playing in the sand beneath.

Tire ladder
Many children can climb this at once. You can climb up the rungs or the tires. Nice and gentle but still inviting children to reach the top. A safe piece of equipment.

Equipment type I b

This group includes equipment with movable parts based on some mechanical principle, such as swings (pendular motion), rocking horses (spring motion), suspension-bridges (swaying motion), carousels and some tractor-tire swings (movement around a center axis), and aerial ropeways (movement caused by a wheel running along a rope). Another kind of equipment which belongs to this group by nature of how it functions is the slide.

Many types of equipment in this group give pleasurable sensations of spinning, speed and dizziness and also provide other sensory experiences to some extent. Such equipment is often popular among children, who enjoy feeling giddy and have a chance under safe conditions to deal with their fear of falling, of exposing themselves to physical danger. Movement is thus combined with a chance for the child to practice overcoming a fear of height and speed, which seems to be important if the child is to have a positive appreciation of himself. Through pleasurable activities he gets to feel that he is master of his body, and it is good for his ego to know that he dares and he can.

Certain equipment such as swings, serves a somewhat different function for younger children than for older ones. The young child enjoys swinging in a safe, secure way. Bigger children often play together, taking turns pushing each other or spinning around. For children ages 7 - 10 swings are often a meeting place where they can sit and talk about what to do. Other

types of equipment are too difficult for little children but are appreciated all the more by older children, such as the aerial ropeway and large suspension-bridge.

Slides, like swings, are appreciated by children of all ages. Our functional studies show that slides bedded in a slope and equipped with sturdy steps are excellent for children from the age of one year up to 10 - 12. Such a slide offers children a chance to play together instead of leading to competition and fighting over who is going to go up first. Moreover, slides attached to a slope involve less risk of injuries. Since equipment in this group is often based on a mechanical principle and includes movable parts, the risk of accidents is considerable. Especially dangerous are carousels. Besides the problem of getting caught in the machinery, the high speeds can cause nausea and there is also a risk of several children ganging up on someone. Both from the viewpoint of safety and function, therefore, those carousels which can reach high speeds should be eliminated, as well as those where one child can prevent another from getting off if he wants to. Another type of potentially dangerous but functionally worthwhile equipment is the seesaw. Here there is a risk of crushing a foot or knee or getting a finger caught in the middle. When it comes to rocking horses on a spring, there are still models in use which carry the risk of getting a finger caught.

Suspension-bridges, which were observed to function well and to have various exciting aspects, involve the danger of getting caught and also, in the case of younger children, of falling down.

A suspension-bridge is often used by a large group of children, at once. It can happen that younger children, those between one and three, slowly and carefully proceed across the bridge, only to have a gang of 5 - 7-year-olds come and begin to run and jump on it, screaming and yelling wildly. The younger children are in danger of falling or being stepped on. It is therefore important to build a suspension-bridge either so that the youngest children cannot get up on it themselves or so that there is something they can grab hold of to keep their balance if necessary.

The aerial ropeway is functionally a very worthwhile piece of equipment. It is appealing to children and stimulates cooperation. Unfortunately, aerial ropeways are often too short to offer real excitement and calculated risk-taking. To be safe, the ropeway must be designed well, especially that part on which the child rides. It is important that the child sit securely, preferably in a vertical or horizontal tire. Holding on with the arms alone is not enough. The braking mechanism is also crucial; it should not cause a jerk since then the child can too easily fall off. It is important that an aerial ropeway can be closed down when something is not working properly. Moreover, as with all equipment, the surface underneath is extremely significant. In the course of our observations we have seen frightening examples of poor placement of such equipment. In particular it must be borne in mind that there is a projectile effect at the end of the track and a child can fall with great speed far from the actual end of the ropeway.

As for slides, which are an excellent type of equipment from a functional standpoint, the greatest danger is that the child can fall down from the highest point. It is above all the old-fashioned sort of slide with ladder which is dangerous. Putting up a sign "for children over 5 only" is hardly

It can be difficult for a young child to hang on if bigger kids come along and start jumping on the bridge.

satisfactory, since children enjoy sliding from quite a **young** age. Much better are slides bedded in a slope. An asphalt hill can be a problem since the smooth surface is often much too slippery in the winter. A grassy hill with foot-holds built into the slope is preferable.

In the case of all the equipment in this group, it is the foundation that is most important for safety. Around swings safety considerations require a fence, and the entry to the swing area should be through a gate. There should be sand at least five meters in front of and behind the swings, since children like jumping while in motion. Swings suspended on long cables require an even larger sand area.

Equipment type I c

This group includes composite equipment with various levels, room-creating elements, steps, roofs, balance beams, slides, suspension-bridges, hammocks, ropes and rope ladders, all of which comprise a unit. To this group belongs equipment ranging from the simple type of house-plus-slide all the way to large complex structures which include most of the above-named elements.

Equipment in this group combines the experience of enclosed spaces and of height with speed and giddiness. In our study we have called all such equipment **combination equipment** since it combines exercise with other functions and, from a developmental viewpoint, fits physical movement into a larger context. Since such equipment contains secluded corners as well as platforms designed so that older children can move around in different ways and with varying degrees of difficulty, it may encourage imaginative and role play and even rule games. Sometimes there are loose parts such as benches which invite experimentation and cooperation. Such equipment is most effective if children have access in their play to big cloths, blankets, planks, bricks, cardboard, buckets, dress-up and other materials to complement the equipment itself.

It isn't any fun when the others ride away from you. This merry-go round on ice has its dangers but it also has the advantage that even an adult can get warmed up taking a turn.

The sturdy double railing increases the safety of this bridge.

Our observations clearly show that at supervised playgrounds loose materials such as bikes, carts, excavators and building blocks easily win out over all the fixed equipment (except possibly swings, slides and sand-pits), even over combination climbing equipment. At unsupervised playgrounds, however, where there are no loose materials, such combination equipment is used to a relatively great extent.

Several manufacturers have taken up and developed the idea of combination equipment. It has become more and more common to sell equipment as a system of components with different variations possible for different settings and age groups. Older children often find equipment more enjoyable the larger it is since it is higher and has more surfaces to move about on. Unlike younger children, older ones are able to comprehend a larger piece of equipment or a system as a unit. This type of equipment has clear advantages over ordinary climbing frames. It is however still **static** in the sense that **it cannot be altered by the children themselves.**

Happily enough, some manufacturers have now begun to realize that children themselves should be able to build and alter their play equipment. Equipment is gradually being developed in which only the basic frame is fixed; all else can easily be assembled by children and adults working together. Unfortunately such equipment will prbably not be available for unsupervised playgrounds. Until we are able to solve the problem of supervision and maintenance at local playgrounds, combination equipment such as we have today is a necessary compromise.

When it comes to safety considerations, nothing special has come up during our observations of type I c equipment that has not already been noted in connection with equipment of types I a and I b.

Since the beams on large combination equipment can easily become icy and dangerous in the winter, such equipment should be dismantled while the weather is cold. This is not really a disadvantage, since the novelty when the equipment is reassembled again enhances its value, and putting together the equipment, with all this can mean for cooperation between children and adults, occurs at least once a year.

This so-called ''ship-wreck'' is too hard for younger children to grasp as a whole and too easy and boring for children old enough to view it as a unit. (Catalogue excerpt)

Play with Variety!

Many types of play equipment function well alone, but a combination of several surely increases the play value. The shipwreck is a carefully thought-out combination of various sturdy parts permanently fixed in the ground which function as an obstacle course providing a lot of exercise.

A plaything suitable for posing . . .
but the reality is something else.

This cement "boat" was not used until someone managed to dig up the mast. Then it became interesting to see if it was possible to climb up without tipping over. (Brandbergen)

Group II: Equipment for pretending, creating and constructing
Equipment type II a

Static representational equipment includes equipment that represents animals or vehicles: pigs, cats, horses, boats, trains, cars. Tree-trunks and sculpture are also included in this group. We have concluded that functionally these have no great value. It is seldom that children actually developed imaginative play around them since they are fixed in the ground, designed to be used in one pathway, and impossible to change. Furthermore, there are seldom any loose materials available at the playground which might stimulate and enrich this type of play.

The equipment of this type that functions best is that which includes some loose parts or is not fastened to the ground and thus can be rolled around and used to represent various things. As for larger pieces of equipment, boats wtih a real mast, railings and steering wheel seem to appeal to children most.

Representational equipment has only in a few cases led to fantasy play such as taking a ride in a boat or car. The decisive factor seems to be which particular experiences a particular group of children has had. At one playground where a leader had actively inspired the children to pretend that they were taking a boat trip, play was full of feeling, whereas at two other playgrounds where no such stimulus was provided, the boats were seldom used and **if** they were used, served only as a place to sit or climb. Probably it is actual discarded vehicles with all their real-life details that are most stimulating. Play sculptures attract children above all because they have functional values similar to those of small combination equipment, that is they are high and include a slide and "rooms."

Most static representational equipment is, in its present form, **dull** and **safe.** Much more exciting vehicles could be provided but would require some extra effort to make sure they were not dangerous. Making such effort would certainly lead to more interesting and engaging symbolic play than that inspired by today's static equipment.

A real-life boat cabin or locomotive with genuine parts stimulates the imagination.

A play sculpture with a distinct character can be a splendid symbol for an area. (Drakenbergsparken)

Equipment type II b

Room-building equipment can, given the right conditions, have a high functional value. It has proved to be the case, however, that such equipment depends very much for its functional value on how it is situated and what loose materials are available. For example, small houses without roofs do **not,** despite what one might expect, inspire children to play make-believe games, but are mostly used for climbing. Judging from our observations, climbing up onto the roof or enjoying the contrast between dark inside and light outside are important experiences which some equipment of this type provides.

The playhouses which function best are those with roof and floor (which can be asphalt - sand floors are unfortunately often used as toilets) and which also have doors and windows. A floor is important since play often involves cleaning up and sweeping. But most important of all in promoting imaginative play is access to loose materials. Only at supervised playgrounds where boxes, buckets, brooms, dress-up clothes, furniture, dolls and teddy bears, wagons, etc. were available did we see boys and girls actually develop fantasy play in playhouses in the way intended.

Another type of room-building equipment, the maze, was used sporadically either by children under three who wandered around inside or

Small houses without roofs are used now and then for climbing. Not even when they are grouped as nicely as they are here, on a wooden slope, are they used for "living in" or playing hide-and-seek. Think if they could be regarded as frameworks for further building! (Husby)
The text in the picture is taken from a catalogue.

Play hut

Climbing frame, Indian tent, lapp hut, house for playing mother-father-child. All in one structure. Sets the child's imagination going and stimulates cooperation. The play hut is made of lay panels which are rugged and stable. No loose parts. The floor makes it usuable all year round. It can be set up easily.

by older children who rode bikes there or used it to fasten a twist rope to for lack of a better place. Storefront props were not observed to function particularly well at local playgrounds as these areas are much to "tidied up" and lack "junk" lying around which can be sold.

Room-building equipment also includes towers and wind and rain shelters. Look-out towers have very different rates of use at different playgrounds. To reach the top and look out are important experiences; children want to overcome the feeling of being little and to find out how high they dare go. The look-out point also has a meaningful social function. From it a child can see who comes to the playground and where his friends are playing. A tower can also be an excellent place to find seclusion and privacy. At the same time, having a number of pieces of static equipment all of which serve as look-outs lined up in a row, as sometimes happens, is entirely unnecessary.

Wind and rain shelters have been found to be a very important feature, especially at playgrounds which lie a bit away from the nearest houses. Such playgrounds usually have no visitors at all in "so-so" weather. Grown-ups who sit still are bothered more by wind and bad weather than children and inclined to retreat indoors quickly, which usually means that small children must follow in also. But if there is a chance to take shelter from a shower then grown-ups are more likely to stay and children get a chance to experience the wonderful water puddles and steaming ground that follow the rain.

As far as safety is concerned, playhouses can involve certain risks if they are high and children are tempted to climb up on the roof. We have seen boys climbing up onto the roof of one playhouse and then jump to the roof of another house near by. When this happens, it is easy for someone to get knocked down. If playhouses are set out in a group it is better if they are far enough apart that children cannot jump between them. This also makes sense from a functional standpoint since wild kinds of play disturb the calm symbolic play that should be going on in connection with playhouses. At the same time, the houses should stand close enough together, and with the openings somewhat facing each other, so that they are experienced as a group, since play often involves children living in different houses and going to visit each other.

Rain shelters also involve certain risks since they are often used for climbing. They should for this reason not stand on a hard surface. At one park the rain shelter had previously been equipped with a climbing net but this had been removed, undoubtedly for reasons of safety. Our observations indicated that this did **not** stop children from climbing but rather challenged them all the more!

Reeds make an excellent play environment. Here children clear them away with home-made scythes so they can build their own tower.
When children build a tower they consider it important to see but not be seen. From this tower they can spy on people going past on the road near by.

Equipment type II c

There are few types of fixed play equipment to be found at playgrounds today which can be included in the group of construction materials. This is unfortunate since equipment of this type satisfies most of the criteria for developing activity as we have defined it. Play with constructive materials often lasts a long time, gives rise to both practice and symbolic play, and invites experimentation and exploration.

What does exist at playgrounds are different kinds of building sets, chests of blocks, and sand-pits. Note that we have defined these as fixed equipment in our study since they have their fixed place at the playground. But in fact, paradoxically enough, the fixed equipment which has proved to function most flexibly is really loose material - namely the sand-pit. Sand is a material which is popular from infancy long up into the school years. Naturally, sand play is enriched greatly if children have access to buckets, shovels, wheelbarrows, excavators, carts, cardboard, cloths and other complementary accessories.

In order for sand-pits to function best they should be protected from wind and rain, and there should be water available for play. Sand should be at least 80 cm deep. (That it is unsuitable to place climbing equipment in sand-pits used for sand play has already been discussed.) Sand-pits with many angles and corners, projecting rocks and backboards or other room-building elements have been observed to function particularly well.

The chest of building blocks is also a type of fixed equipment that in many ways is really loose material. It provides a good example of how construction materials can be used with pleasure by children at different stages of development and for different purposes. Two-year-olds lug around the blocks and throw them out of the chest while five-year-olds build themselves sofas or tables for use in their make-believe play. An eight-year-old, on the other hand, may use the long pieces as a track for a wheelbarrow. Because children can change and shape construction materials themselves and follow their own creative impulses, play is continually refreshed and stimulated by their availability.

When it comes to the safety aspects of construction equipment, these do not have so much to do with design or surface. Instead it is the interaction between children and grown-ups that is important. Adults have a responsibility to teach children to use and master such materials. They must teach children, for example, that fire is dangerous but that, if one is careful, it can be an obedient and useful servant, useful to burn refuse, keep warm, cook food and even fire pottery. It is important that the child have a chance to experience such processes if he is to be able to understand and master his world. Finding out about water, growing things, chemical and physical properties, about everything that is living and changing requires close teamwork between those with and without experience, if our cultural heritage is to be passed on. When one keeps all this in mind, then one can better understand that safety precautions are of somewhat secondary importance.

To think about

Much fixed play equipment is not used by children. It is therefore necessary to find other ways to satisfy the need children have to move about, to pretend, to experience a variety of sensory impressions and also to explore, influence and take responsibility for their environment and to be useful to others.

It is only in exceptional cases, moreover, that fixed equipment satisfies the need grown-ups have for outdoor activity. Grown-ups do not come outside unless there is something for them to do that makes sense or some place where it is pleasant to sit.

If one chooses to have fixed equipment as a complement to, or perhaps compensation for, other aspects of the play environment, the following points should be borne in mind:

- Equipment intended to function as a gathering place should be situated where people in the area naturally congregate.
- Equipment intended for intense imaginative play in small groups should be placed in a calm but not isolated section of the playground, with access to loose materials, bushes with various kinds of leaves and berries, natural terrain with pine cones, stones, bark, sticks, gravel and water, and with somewhere children can store what they find, i.e. some kind of play chest.
- Large fixed equipment intended to be used by bigger children for vigorous physical play should be situated so that it does not disturb fantasy play but so that younger children can watch older children at play.
- Equipment which is obviously unsuitable for young children should be designed so that they **cannot** get up on it.
- Equipment should be selected and situated so that it can be used by children ages 1 - 12. The playground should be able to accommodate the changing needs and skills of children.
- Equipment intended to be used by small children should be complemented by a comfortable place for grown-ups to sit nearby.
- Equipment should be grouped together with items in the existing setting, such as a playhouse with a rock or tree stump or other complementary equipment. "Even spacing" of fixed equipment is objectionable as is an accumulation of equipment in large sand areas. Natural groupings with some form of screening provided by differences in level, fences or bushes create the best play possibilities.
- Fixed equipment should be chosen so that there is a certain variety among the different play facilities in a residential area.
- It is better to have a **few** pieces of equipment offering different types of play for different age groups than to have lots of equipment all serving the same function.

15
Loose Play Equipment - Something To Do Something With

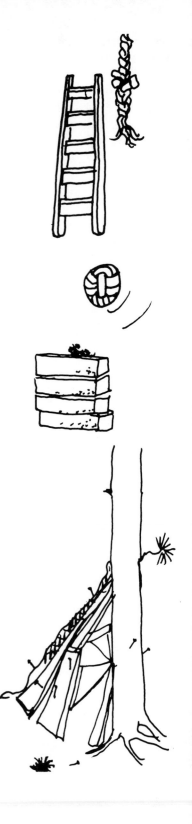

Loose materials are of crucial significance in enriching play. This is entirely natural since the chances to vary how something is used obviously increase when materials can be moved about and changed.

Materials which invite physical exercise

In **practice play** the use of such supplementary materials as ropes, ladders, hammocks, and netting can vary the experience of climbing on trees and fixed equipment. In this way the activity of climbing can be continually renewed and made interesting.

Wagons, carts, cars and bikes provide ways to move, and this is fun in itself. Moreover, such equipment often encourages children to cooperate and play together. One child rides towards and away from the others. Or children ride together, push each other, compete. Or a child can play alone for awhile, enjoying the feeling of speed, balance and increased dexterity.

A classic example of movable play equipment is the ball. The uses to which a ball can be put are endless, from simple training of the ability to throw and roll a ball, to more social forms, then to **rule play** with complicated rules, and finally on to adult sports. Soccer, tennis, hockey, and golf can continue to be fascinating for years and years. The chances for variety are great and ball play requires skill and the ability to follow rules and to understand all the moves and tricks of one's teammates and opponents.

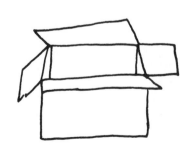

Materials for pretending, creating and constructing

The loose materials needed if **symbolic play** is to develop include objects with a simple form which the child can imagine to be whatever he wishes, as well as certain fundamental materials which the child can shape after his own intentions and fantasies, such as cardboard, wood, cloth, rope, stones, gravel, sand, snow, water, etc.

What the child creates with such materials is used in play to replace something real. Thus a boat made out of bark can represent a real boat which the child has seen; in his play he can dream he is captain or deal with his fears that the boat might sink.

What the child makes himself can also serve as a precursor and basis for his future mental development, his ability to think abstractly. When a child makes a clay pot, he learns the meaning of such concepts as inside, outside, full and empty which he will later be able to use without needing to have a concrete object before him.

Other kinds of material help the child to "become" someone else, as when a red hat and a rope change the child into a fireman answering an alarm, or a purse and gloves make a "fine lady." In this way the child has a chance to practice different adult roles.

Loose materials - an essential complement to fixed equipment

A lot of equipment and room-creating units like playhouses are meant to stimulate the imagination and encourage symbolic play. For this to happen, it seems necessary that the child have loose objects to complement the equipment. A static wooden pig **can perhaps** be fun if one has a bucket with grass and water and maybe some boards to build a sty. A playhouse or a store-front obviously requires furnishings and things to sell. Often it is only very simple materials which are needed, but **without** these play does not develop. It should be as obvious that loose, "untidy" things are needed for symbolic play as it is that a ball is needed to play soccer.

According to our observations, loose materials seem to be much more effective than fixed equipment in encouraging children to work and play together. This is confirmed by one of the forerunners in the field of children's social development, Mildred Parten, in a study made in 1932. Parten discovered that the quality and quantity of social interactions were influenced by the play materials the child was using. With the help of a mathematical model she calculated the social value of a number of different play items. She found that materials encouraging some form of role-play, like houses and dolls, gave rise to the most complex forms of play, namely cooperative play.

Children are scavengers

A common feature at the playgrounds we have studied is that loose materials proved to be of crucial significance in enriching and refreshing play. All children seem to be scavengers like Astrid Lindgren's Pippi Longstocking. Our notes are full of examples of this. At Brandbergen we saw children fight over an empty cardboard box while all the fixed equipment stood unused. On another occasion we watched children making a kite out of a plastic grocery bag and some string. Dry clumps of earth were used to draw a hopscotch on the pavement. A grocery cart left in a play yard for some time in the fall and spring was used by children to give each other rides or just push around. At Stamgardsparken an empty beer can became a ball for a bored three-year-old. When this happened, his mother "woke up" and fetched a real ball for him. A 5- or 6-year old girl at the same playground used a beer can to scoop up sand and pour it over the asphalt, thereby turning herself into a kind of dump truck. Even at Tingvalla it happened several times that children used empty beer cans in their play. Once a loose board from a bike was laid over a stump by two boys about five and became a seesaw! At Bellman park a boy put on a mask while using the slide and down came a **monster** to the horror of all the others! At the same place four children, ages 4-5, kept busy hoisting up buckets of sand onto the roof of a playhouse, using a rope they found. Some children filled the bucket, others raised and lowered it. The children got the idea of emptying the sand between the slots of the roof so that it ran down like rain.

Grocery carts are one of the few movable items children can find at today's playgrounds. Otherwise the outdoor environment is tidy. All too tidy. (Brandbergen)

The word "toilet" has been painted above the entrance to this hut.

Two boys in Nyby rode on a sled they found. They took turns and laughed a great deal. The one whose turn it was to watch had as much fun as his friend on the sled.

A three-year-old boy at Vårdaren, a new housing area in Råcksta in Stockholm, kept busy for an hour and a half hitting a soccer ball around with a hockey club. Another boy, about 4 years' old, spent an entire morning and afternoon at Tessin play park in central Stockholm rolling a car down an inclined wooden plane time and time again, then riding down himself in a cart. A six-year-old girl with her two cousins, ages 3 - 4, was at the playground in Fisksätra one stormy day. She crept under the fence into the carpentry area, took a few loose boards and set them over the window and door openings of the small roofed playhouse. All three were delighted that they could shut themselves in from the wind and that it was dark inside. In Tingvalla two girls ages 5- 6 collected bottles and cans from the litter baskets to use for playing store, which was the only time we saw the storefronts there being used. In Barrsätra in Sandviken a steel jungle-gym was used as the start of a little house which two boys, 4 and 6, built out of pieces of board. When they were urged to tear down the structure because it might be dangerous, they built another one against the bar. At other times these two pieces of fixed equipment were rarely used.

It has also happened that children have made use of natural materials in their play. The playground in Fisksätra is located partly on a wooded hill. There children use materials taken from nature when playing in the man-made creek. One time some sticks together with litter such as bits of wood and plastic bags became a house and dam between the rocks in the creek. Several children peeled bark from the trees to serve as boats. In Stamgardsparken two boys ages 8 or 9 were able, with the help of a movable litter basket, to take sand and fill up a puddle at the bottom of the slide which had kept children from being able to go down it.

Bushes often provide both places and materials for playing. At the entrances in an older residential area in Flysta, Spånga, there are bushes which, from a child's viewpoint, are enormous, growing so that there are hollow spaces in the middle while the high hanging branches cut off the view. Once under these bushes "lived" three girls, 5 - 6 years' old, in a "three-room apartment." They were sitting and eating "dinner" on plastic plates consisting of three sorts of fruit and berries. On some of the branches they had hung out "the wash." Outside a tractor and doll buggy stood in a neat row. "Mother and child" and "a visiting aunt" sometimes went out to shop for more food, i.e. they picked more berries from the bushes.

It is important that bushes and shrubs at playgrounds are not prickly and inhospitable. It is exciting to be able to hide among the bushes, make "paths", play tag, etc.

The following scene was observed in Orrhammaren in Årsta in Stockholm, also an older neighborhood with thick vegetation. It is autumn and the leaves are golden. Three children dash from the swings to a shrub, run around a little, creep into the bushes. A girl, about six, suggests that they play cops and robbers. They sit in the dense bushes and collect yellow leaves in plastic bags and talk about a rabbit that they saw once before in the same place. They sneak around in the bushes hiding from each other. They talk about the rabbit. Then one boy says he is going to "stick" the rabbit, i.e. draw some blood, see if it is a healthy or sick rabbit. After a bit the children creep out and proudly show their bags full of leaves to the rabbit and then ask mother for more bags.

In a hilly wooded area with ditches and hollows, puddles formed in the rain can lead to imaginative games in which children use materials found in the woods for playing in the water. In Högbergsparken, a local play area in Uppsala, two 6-year-old boys, were observed playing in a water-filled ditch, using sticks as boats.

Such things are what we have **seen.** You can surely add many examples from your own observation and experience that further prove what an "appetite" children have for "things to do something with" when they play. One of our observers noted the following incident on an island out in Stockholm's archipelago:

"On Resarö last summer I saw a group of children, 8- 9-years' old, trying to drag along a large log which they had found by the side of the road. They struggled to get it up on a wagon so they could take it down to the beach. They had decided to build a raft.

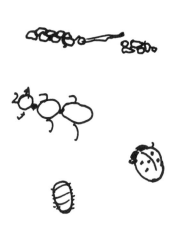

In a shrub you can hide away and think, look at small creepy things and let your imagination loose. (Orrhammaren)

The children struggled for several hours with the log but did not succeed. The idea of making a raft survived this failure however, and eventually they found some lighter boards and logs. With the help of some blocks of frigolite which they found on the beach and some strong ropes, boards and nails which they got from grown-ups, they succeeded after a week's work in building a raft. At first they put the floating blocks on top of the boards but then realized that was not so good. So they put them under the boards, and that was better. Building the raft was accompanied by a great deal of intense discussion. Many suggestions were made; some were discarded, others tried out. To get the raft finished, everyone's help was needed and the children were able to agree on what alternatives to try. When the big day came and the raft was done, the whole gang went out, dressed up as pirates, to discover new worlds!

The children did not get any direct help from adults, but no one stopped them either. Materials such as hammers and nails were provided by parents, and the rest they found themselves at the beach or in the woods. The grown-ups recalled their own childhood while watching their children at work. A common sort of remark was "This is how children should play . . ." or "This is how it used to be!" The parents remembered that they themselves played like this once. All who passed by where the children were working were interested, asked how things were going, and sometimes gave advice."

More variety in areas with low-rise housing

In the case of local play areas, we have found that it is very common for children to bring along playthings from home. Where the surrounding buildings **have been low** and the playground very accessible, children have gone back and forth after more things as they were needed. The supply of play materials is thus more varied in such areas than it is at playgrounds adjacent to high-rise buildings and at unsupervised parks located some distance away from the residential area. The types of materials which are common at playgrounds in low-rise areas include small cars, balls, dolls, doll clothes, blankets. buggies, tricycles, tractors, pedal cars, bikes, simple things for playing dress-ups, jump ropes, string and kites. A 6-year-old boy at Vårdaren, a playground in Råcksta in Stockholm, is not allowed to play cars with two other boys because only taxis are allowed on their roads. He rushes immediately into the house to get a taxi and is then allowed to play. Another time at the same playground there is a wonderful water puddle after a rainstorm. Three children come to the playground, but two turn back at once. "Wait, I'm just going to get my rubber boots!" When they come out again all three play in the water with boats which they push with long sticks.

At local playgrounds next to high-rise buildings and at unsupervised playgrounds to which one goes for a special outing, the children often bring a small supply of simple toys with them. Mothers, or the children themselves, have a bag with buckets, shovels, and molds or an assortment of cars. Children at such playgrounds cannot follow through so easily on their spontaneous play ideas but must play with what is there. An example from Tingvalla shows, however, that this system of taking things along in a bag can have its advantages. A 5-6-year-old girl packed an extremely varied assortment of cans, molds, bowls, plates and boxes of all different shapes. Together with some other children she played that she was "baking." The great variety and the novelty of the things the girl had with her even interested a boy who had earlier been unruly and aggressive. Unfortunately it is very seldom that children have with them toys for sand play that exhibit much variety. Mostly what they have is plastic, in standard shapes; rarely have we noticed a wooden spoon or baking form. This is true despite the fact that children clearly notice details which distinguish one bucket from another, for example. This delight in identifying and distinguishing should be encouraged by giving children several sorts of materials and more varied shapes to use when playing. Easiest and best is to use everyday items found in the home.

A chest for playthings

It would be desirable if children and parents had more chance to leave playthings at the playground. Nearly every yard in Sweden has a large container which holds sand for use in the winter time. We suggest that an excellent idea would be to place a second container beside the one marked SAND and label it THINGS FOR PLAY. This could be a project for parents and children to work on together. The residents in the area could contribute discarded items and the children could play with them for a while before they were thrown away for good. Someone would, of course, need to see to it that the play area did not become too messy and that anything dangerous was eliminated. The advantage of such a system is that children would get new and interesting things to play with, investigate, take apart, and make something from and the playground would become a more exciting place. It would be good if each yard could have one secluded corner which was allowed to be a mess, with playthings strewn about. The overall impression of tidiness would be maintained if such a corner were hidden by some fencing and quickgrowing bushes. Perhaps you yourself remember some hidden corner you had as a child which no adult was allowd to disturb?

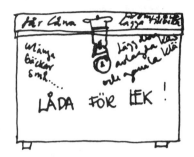

One sign that a play area functions as an extension of the home is that children dare to leave their toys behind when they go in.

More variety with play leaders

At the larger supervised playgrounds we have studied, loose materials are used very much more than fixed equipment. The most illuminating example of this comes from Hallonbergen where the combination climbing-sliding structure was used now and then before loose materials such as bikes and carts were taken out for the spring. After these things were available, however, they put the fixed equipment out of business, and in fact were so much in demand that a waiting list was necessary. A similar situation occurred in Upplands-Väsby and in Orminge. In Upplands-Väsby much of the fixed equipment is always empty. When bikes and carts are taken out, they even win out over the more exciting equipment up in the woods - the suspension-bridge, high slide, tower and aerial ropeway.

At the playground Geijers in the center of Uppsala, which is only staffed in the summer and where children seldom bring along anything of their own, the combination climbing frame is used more than at Hallonbergen. Still, the use decreases, according to the personnel, during the summer. It seems that large combination equipment is used more when the alternative of playing with loose materials does not exist.

We can conclude from what has been said here that wheeled toys of all kinds - bikes, scooters, big and little tricycles, wagons, carts and cars - are well used at playgrounds and that asphalt, especially if it slopes somewhat and has some bumpy spots, is an excellent surface for playing with these **vehicles**. Children play both alone and with others. They explore how the vehicle works and try out their balance, strength and courage. Play together

The best fun of all is when you help build a car yourself. A discarded baby buggy provides a fine start.

often becomes symbolic play, like playing horse and wagon, bus, etc. Vehicles are used from the age of two up to about ten, depending on the design. It is common for younger and older children to play with them together.

Children who play at supervised playgrounds use more **different** types of materials in their play and seem to prefer the materials provided by the playground to anything else. Tables 3 and 4 indicate the number of different items which children of different ages have been observed to use at supervised and unsupervised playgrounds in the spring. The materials have been divided into the following groups: Prefabricated playthings brought along by the children, found objects (i.e. "junk") and objects belonging to the playground's supplies.

At all the playgrounds which provide children with loose play materials such as balls, stilts, high-jump apparatus, carts, bikes, excavators, hammers and other tools, pedal cars, dolls, and doll buggies, it is primarily these that the children have used. When it comes to the number of prefabricated things brought along by children from home, there is a large degree of variation. The number of different objects was lower at supervised than at unsupervised playgrounds. The figures for prefabricated materials at supervised playgrounds are probably somewhat exaggerated since it is difficult to tell if buckets, shovels, small cars, and the like have been brought from home or belong to the playground. These types of playthings have consistently been counted in the group of prefabricated objects brought by the children.

The use in play of "found objects" or "junk" such as sticks, paper bags, string, rocks, forgotten sleds or grocery carts, dandelions, grass and earthworms varies from place to place depending on the availability of such material. The use of such things does not seem to decrease, however, because children have access to "nice" toys.

Table 15-1. Children at these **unsupervised** playgrounds have been observed to use the following number of different play materials.

Play materials at playgrounds without play leaders	Age group				
	1-3	3-5	5-7	7-10	10-13
Fältöversten					
brought from home, prefab	-	4	4	5	-
found objects	-	1	1	2	-
supplied by the playground	-	1	-	-	-
Total	(-)	6	5	7	(-)
Brandbergen					
brought from home, prefab	-	9	6	2	2
found objects	-	3	5	1	-
supplied by the playground	-	-	-	-	-
Total	(-)	12	11	3	2
Tingvalla					
brought from home, prefab	2	6	11	5	3
found objects	2	8	7	3	1
supplied by the playground	-	-	-	-	-
Total	4	14	18	8	4
Bellman					
brought from hom, prefab	-	9	7	4	-
found objects	-	3	3	1	-
supplied by the playground	-	-	1	1	1
Total	(-)	12	11	6	(1)
Average number	-	11	11	6	-
Average total (all ages): 30					

Table 15-2. Children at these **supervised** playgrounds have been observed to use the following number of different play materials.

Play materials at playgrounds with play leaders	Age group				
	1-3	3-5	5-7	7-10	10-13
Fisksätra					
brought from home, prefab	1	2	2	4	-
found objects	-	-	2	1	-
supplied by the playground	-	2	7	3	-
Total	(1)	(4)	11	8	(-)
Orminge					
brought from home, prefab	2	4	2	-	-
found objects	-	5	2	2	-
supplied by the playground	5	11	10	11	2
Total	7	20	14	13	2
Hallonbergen					
brought from home, prefab	3	2	5	-	1
found objects	1	-	1	-	-
supplied by the playground	5	7	10	-	1
Total	9	9	16	(-)	2
Nyby					
brought from home, prefab	5	6	6	1	-
found objects	4	5	4	4	-
supplied by the playground	4	7	7	10	5
Total	13	18	17	15	5
Upplands-Väsby					
brought from home, prefab	4	6	8	2	1
found objects	1	2	4	5	-
supplied by the playground	1	8	9	7	1
Total	6	16	21	14	2
Average number	8,7	15	18	12	-
Average total (all ages): 50					

If we add up the number of different play materials used at the playgrounds, we find that the average for all ages together at unsupervised playgrounds is about 30, and at supervised playgrounds about 50. This indicates that children at a supervised playground have more to choose from. We can also see that the average number of different play materials used by children of different ages is consistently greater at supervised playgrounds. This is most striking in the case of children 5 - 10. For children 7 - 10 there is on the average twice as many choices of materials at supervised playgrounds.

Examples of how some
loose materials function

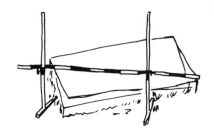

One type of loose material that has proved to be very popular is **high-jump equipment**, which was used frequently by children from the age of five up into the teens. Since the child can himself regulate the degree of difficulty, from just jumping on the mat to jumping over the bar at different heights and with different styles, this equipment can retain its excitement as children grow older.

The chest of blocks is another diligently used and very popular material. It can be enjoyed by children from the ages of one up to thirteen. The youngest mostly use the whole chest. They sit in it, build in and around it. They are also amused by the resistance which the blocks offer, since they are sufficiently heavy to make it an interesting "job" to throw them all out of the chest.

Children a little bigger, from five up, build both in and outside the container. Since the chest and its blocks have not set form they can be used after the children's own wishes. A 5 - 6-year-old boy in Hallonbergen emptied everything out of one of the chests. Then he built himself a bed out of blocks and a night table beside it. He also made a little stove. He was proud of his little house and eager for the play leader to come and take a look at it.

The blocks can also be used in other parts of the playground. In Fisksätra a girl of about six built two chairs and a table in the playhouse using these blocks.

Other popular loose materials at supervised parks are movable seesaws, stilts and various board games as well as ball games like land hockey and soccer. Board games are especially important as a means of promoting social interaction. Children sit still for awhile and talk calmly with each other and with the play leaders.

Loose materials that are popular but not so common are hobby-horses, roller skates, large cloths and ropes. In Hallonbergen the staff got the idea of enriching the children's "horse play" by embroidering common horse names on the bridles of the hobby-horses. The result was that the children energetically played horse and wagon, using the small children's play enclosure as the stable. At Spångaby, a play park in Spånga, two boys ages 3 - 4 had a stable with hobby-horses in a hollow tree. Two boys, ages 2 and 4, at Haren, a play park on Söder in Stockholm, put together two hockey goals to form a house and lived there with their horses. Four boys ages 5 - 6, playing at the same park, pretended that a slide next to a wall was a stall.

It is obvious that it does not take much to stimulate symbolic play. A **tarpaulin** makes it possible for children to screen off an area and create a room. At Haren children built a tent in the small children's enclosure next to some bushes. They brought along some toys and played house. Another time some children used a large cloth to create a private place under the jungle-gym next to the wall. Then, using some ropes which they fastened between the slide and a tree trunk, they "tied up their boat." The ropes were also used for lifting things up onto the jungle-gym.

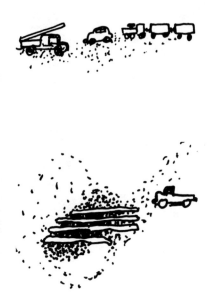

Cars, cars, cars

At all types of playgrounds, children play with small cars. We believe that one reason cars are so popular is that they are so carefully and realistically made that it is interesting to notice their design. To know what distinguishes one model from another is stimulating and can lead to much discussing and comparing. Cars are as omnipresent in our society as the horse was for earlier generations of children, who made their own horses of pine cones and sticks. Cars make noise and give off fumes and are impossible to avoid. Moreover, a large percentage of families with small children have a car, so that the car is a part of the child's everyday reality. The grown-up who drives a car must be skillful. The child sees the grown-up in action when he is driving. It is with the help of cars, buses, trains and boats that the child travels to a favorite grandparent or other exciting places. Cars can be a stimulus to the imagination and they can be included in play that encompasses a larger context as well, one that gradually includes the exhaust from cars and other drawbacks. Cars, in other words, are an essential part of children's lives. So it is not strange that many children today are "crazy over cars."

Grasping technical complexities

One type of loose equipment which we have observed to be popular wherever available is **excavators.** These are used regularly by children from the age of three and up and lead to exploration of how the machine functions, to simple practice play, and to symbolic play where the excavator is used in a larger context. In Brandbergen a boy had taken out his own excavator, which was the same type as those which the play park had available. Using it, he filled the wagon behind a tricycle which two other boys were playing with. They drove away to another sand-pit and dumped out their load, then raced back for more. They played at "working" and they worked hard. The rest of the children present and a mother had nothing else to do so they watched this game.

Because of their design and their popularity, excavators seem to encourage cooperation. We have noticed several times that a conflict over an excavator has been resolved by the children deciding to cooperate instead. This requires that there be complementary equipment available such as carts and shovels. Once in Nyby two boys, 5 - 6 years' old, wanted to have the excavator that a younger boy was using. The younger boy did not want to give it up and the older boys then hit on the idea of having him load up their wagons instead. In this way, all three boys could play together. Another time in Nyby two boys took turns operating the excavator and filling it with the help of a shovel. The boys played that they were real "workmen." Their play was probably inspired by the fact that construction work was going on at a school nearby and children had a chance to see workmen in action.

The design of the excavaor is very close to the "real thing" which naturally gives an extra stimulus to the imagination. To encourage children to play alongside or with each other, there should be several excavators out

and the sand-pit should also be supplied with shovels and carts. The excavator is a type of equipment that is fascinating to young children and that continues to interest children through the years until they have entirely mastered it.

The excavator has many characteristics which one could well wish for in more play materials. We recommend that all who are involved in designing playthings keep it in mind as a model. Surely one could have other playthings that take their inspiration from some mechanical-technical principle, such as a block-and-tackle or machines built on the idea of the lever like plows, dredges, farm and road-building equipment.

Different kinds of mechanically driven lifting and elevator devices are also possible. In general how power derived from an energy source can be used to do work like moving a train forward or lifting a bucket from a well is exciting to explore. Water play can be enriched with pumps and hoses so that children get a chance to learn how a water tower functions. With the help of a water wheel, children can learn about the principle of generating electricity. Pumps and hoses are also good for getting running water into a playhouse or for playing fireman. This kind of exploring does not require access to playthings in the traditional sense. A visit to a hardware store or a scrap dealer may be just the place to start!

• *Playing with an excavator often leads to cooperation.*
• *A mirror or real life.*

Making up things to do yourself

There is a great lack of creative materials at our playgrounds. The youngest children have the sand-pit which gives them a lot of chance to pour sand in and out, build the simple forms which are adequate for their ideas at this stage. The sand-pit is popular and is used through the early school years, i.e. up to about nine. But, while sand is good for building roads, houses, paths and tunnels, it does not do for more sophisticated creations. What is lacking is a variety of materials, such as cardboard, string, cloth, pipes and "waste products" in general which children can make into something using their imagination. In some places there are carpentry corners or other building materials such as large blocks. But a few carpentry corners here and there are not enough. Children must be able to generate and develop such play themselves. If they begin with building a house there should be the chance for this to lead naturally to painting and furnishing it. Cups and saucers are put in rows on the shelves, a rug laid on the floor and some flowers planted round about. One must go to the pump for water to tend the flowers and fix the meals. If only the materials and the freedom to do whatever one wants are there - and this includes being shielded from those who would interfere with such activities - the play of this type can continuously grow and develop and be renewed.

Forward with recycling!

The only one of society's waste products that we regularly use today at our playgrounds are old tires. In the literature on playgrounds, there are abundant suggestions of other materials which could be used: cable spools, pipes of different sizes and materials, barrels, locks, wooden blocks, tractor tires, inner tubes, bricks, stone blocks, etc. There is plenty of room for ingenuity here. What is absolutely clear is that we must give back to children what we have taken away from them, things which with a little imagination they can make something out of. If we do not do this we will bring up children who already when young are passive consumers demanding entertainment rather than active individuals with a creative relationship to the world around them. There is no time to lose. The impoverishment of today's play environments can have devastating consequences, not just in the form of "destruction" today but - what is worse - in terms of the quality of our society, tomorrow.

16
Play Without Materials

In this book it is easy because of our eagerness to emphasize the importance of loose materials compared to fixed play equipment, to exaggerate the important of **materials** in general as a prerequisite for play. In order to restore the balance somewhat, it seems worthwhile to mention that there are many games where **the body itself** is the starting point and object of the game. The very first games of all are of this kind. Mother and father, the child's first playmates, play with the child's body, counting toes or playing "this little piggy", tickling the tummy or planting kisses all over. Such games give the child the feeling that his parents **like** his body, that he is fine and exactly as he should be. Play changes as the child grows older; he is lifted high up, rocked, swung about, turned upside down. The child feels pleasant and giddy. It is nice to be little and a little bit afraid but still safe in the arms of a grown-up. Many types of equipment later take over these functions. The child is rocked (swings), hurled forward (aerial ropeway), suspended upside down (bar, trapeze). The mastery of one's own body, which is basic to a feeling of security and self-identity, is achieved to a large extent through those types of play where the child accomplishes some feat, coordinates his movements perfectly and gradually becomes sure of himself. In many forms of play, being together with others is the most important aspect, while the activity itself is less relevant. Play without materials is often of this type, relating to others being what really matters.

A gang of boys played war on the grassy slope. One pretended to attack. The others rolled down the hill. (Bellman)

Wrestling, playing at being a horse or dog, clapping hands and saying nursery rhymes, playing leap-frog, carrying each other piggy-back, practicing hand-stands with another's help, turning cart-wheels, playing statues, all are wonderful and important games which require soft surfaces and perhaps a little stimulation from older children and grown-ups to get them started. We have seen examples of this type of play, as when children wrestled in the only equipment-free stretch of sand in Brandbergen or rolled down the grassy hill or pretended to trip over a hole. Open surfaces, both hard and soft, are essential for this type of social play.

There are some studies and reports available which suggest that children play together more when they have **few** playthings. Gunilla Dahlberg, a child psychologist active at the Teachers' College in Stockholm, gives an account of some interesting findings along these lines in her report *Playing Together* (1973). In one study of the influence of different play materials and play activities on children's free play, it was found that children spent the longest time in creative play and using manipulative materials and books. Building and carpentry had the highest level of activity and playing alone was most common, since children played most with manipulative material and books. Dramatic play stimulated the greatest amount of playing together.

In another study it was found that children make more social contacts if there are not too many playthings around to draw interest away from playmates. A play environment with only a moderate amount of play equipment, in other words, seems to promote socializing moreover. When equipment is too orderly and well-arranged, there is less scope for children to create and experiment freely.

That play without materials more often leads children to play together with each other is an observation that has been made regarding play among Chinese children. Many visitors to China have described the physical environment at child centers as quite barren, while on the other hand the relationships among the children are rich and of prime importance.

17
Space For Play

Children need to move about

Children need a lot of space for playing. They are constantly in motion. Because their nerves and muscles are growing and developing, they have to change position often. Moreover, their movements are larger than those of adults, who have a controlled, "economical" way of moving. They need more space to "brake" and to take a swing around a corner. To achieve greater precision they must practice over and over again, which is what they do when they play. All this requires **open space.**

Finding space

When it comes to the matter of space, we believe that in our study we have observed an important phenomenon. Space has to do not only with size but also with variety and use. It seems that the child's experience of spaciousness, of having enough space to play, depends to a large extent on the choices which a particular environment provides. In Brandbergen, for example, there is so much equipment that there is no room to kick a ball around, nor is there any suitable place for attaching a twist rope. Children must play soccer in the small grassy area at the bottom of the hill using two sticks as goal-posts, and despite the fact that the playground is large they must go outside it to a carpetbeating rack to find two poles at the right distance from each other to use for playing three-corner twist. The entire playground is taken up with sand, asphalt paths and a grassy hill, and the sand is cluttered with low jungle-gyms. It is not so strange that a boy of about eight told us that his first wish was to flatten out the grassy hill so there would be somewhere to play soccer.

At Vårdaren, a local playground in Råcksta in Stockholm, the children have a problem finding the space they need for soccer practice. They have solved this by playing on a "small scale" with a tennis ball using a small bar as goal. At Tingvalla, which has a large grass area, there is plenty of room for soccer but not for land hockey. However, a **small** asphalt field has been fixed up in the middle of the playground next to the backboard. This small field is used intensively and does more to make the playground feel spacious than if the grass area were to be made much, much larger. It is the sense of having some place to do what is of interest at the moment that creates the feeling of spaciousness.

Many of the rule games played by older children require, first of all, **space.** Sometimes it is a hilly area with a lot of hiding places that is needed. Other activities, such as ball games and jump rope, need large level spaces.

Even the youngest child, one just learning to walk, is challenged by open spaces. Children of this age like to go exploring. What they need are reasonably large areas, preferably with some variation in slope and surface, where they have a chance to go some distance and still be within view of a grown-up.

The feeling of spaciousness, then, is not a simple consequence of having a lot of space, but rather a result of what the space contains, how it is planned, and how much variety there is.

Too little space means more conflicts

A certain amount of research has been done into the influence that the size of a space has on children's play and social behavior. Gunilla Dahlberg (*Playing Together,* 1973) cites several such studies. The methodology usually followed is to observe children playing freely in situations where the amount of available play space varies and then to study the effect of these variations. Such studies show that children have a greater tendency to play alone if the play area is **reduced.** Moreover, the number of conflicts **increases** if there is too little room to play. One researcher emphasizes that an overcrowded play area causes tensions which in their turn disturb and inhibit play. Another researcher confirms this, adding that small play areas cause physical and psychological inhibitions since the children's activity is continually being interrupted. Given this situation the child often isolates himself from others in order to decrease the social pressure and avoid far too insistent external stimuli. In still another study it is stated that children have more physical contact with each other if the density (number of children per square meter) is not too high. The conclusion of all these investigations is that the social pattern of children's play seems to depend more on the size of the play area than on the child's wish to play alone or together with others.

It can therefore be claimed that children need ample space for play and that children play more spontaneously, more often with others, and with more physical contact the larger the space they have to move about in. Too little room creates conflicts and causes children to withdraw inside themselves and play alone.

Being able to play undisturbed

We have seen earlier in this book that different playgrounds vary greatly in the opportunities they give children to play undisturbed in small groups. In Hallonbergen or Orminge for example (and also Upplands-Väsby, Sandvik, Bellman and others) it was possible to take a walk through the whole playground and observe children in groups or alone absorbed in their play. At other playgrounds, however, like Brandbergen or Fältöversten, the pattern was mostly different. Here children wandered around looking for something to do. At Fältöversten, where children ran in and out of the entries and grown-ups often passed by, play was frequently interrupted. The size of the group kept changing and it was necessary to keep starting over. Also at Brandbergen it was seldom that a group of children could play undisturbed by others. Instead, there were many who hurried up and competed over what some other child was already playing with. Another pattern we observed was that many children with nothing to do just stood around and watched those children who were busy playing.

Such observations can be taken as additional proof that space in itself is not enough to create the feeling of spaciousness. It is also necessary to design the play environment so that children have a chance to play undisturbed in small groups. A play area, furthermore, should not be isolated from all contact with adults, but it should not be a kind of thoroughfare either where children are never left in peace to finish what they start. In planning the play environment it is important to try to allow for a wide range of options, permitting both positive, voluntary interactions with others (home, play park house, local playground) and freely-chosen solitude (woods, shrubs, playhouse, playroom).

This rock, which was not blasted away due to lack of money, has proved to be a positive feature of this play area. (Play park near Haren on Söder in Stockholm)

18
Variety Is Important!

To promote children's development as much as possible, a playground should be as full of variety as nature itself. If we could offer children woods, a meadow or a bench we would not need to **plan** for play. How is the child's development affected by the physical setting and what is meant by "promoting" development?

This is a subject we have touched on previously. When Piaget speaks of development he does not use the word in the narrow sense of teaching children a specific skill like reading, nor does he mean that a child's development should be speeded up so that a five-year-old functions like a seven-year-old. On the contrary, Piaget believes that it is important that the child lives entirely and fully at that level of development which he has currently reached. It is impossible, for example, to force a small child with his egocentric way of thinking to function socially and take others into consideration. This would have just the opposite of the desired effect; the child unable to give full expression to his egocentric needs can get stuck at this level and be handicapped in the future regarding his feelings for others. What is important therefore is to give the child **broad experiences** at each level of development. A child who has just learned to walk should be able to practice not only on the parquet floor at home, but on many different surfaces. At that stage at which a child is interested in exploring round objects, it is not enough to have a ball. The round shape occurs also in the cylinder, ring, and semi-circle. A cheek, a berry, a tire swing also have roundness. The child's environment needs to contain an endless amount of **variety** to promote development in the true sense. Piaget states further that breadth of experience is a requirement for establishing firm mental concepts which can later be transformed and used abstractly.

In order for an environment to satisfy these demands for variety, it is essential that it can be changed by those who use it. The human being is characterized by the fact that he is not only influenced strongly by the environment, he can also actively change this environment himself and is thus partially responsible for his own development.

Ground cover

We have seen many examples of how good it is if children have access to **different** types of surfaces at a playground. The best situation is one which provides sand, gravel, grass and asphalt, and even rocks, boulders, woods, meadows, muddy puddles and mounds of stones. Unpaved ground is a very important element in the child's environment, as an example from Vårdaren, a local playground in Råcksta in Stockholm, clearly illustrates. Some children (four boys ranging in age from five to ten years' old) gathered around a puddle which had formed under the "Shipwreck" equipment. They played with boats there and then one boy of about eight hit on the idea of getting some new-mown grass from a near-by slope. With the help of a younger boy he drove a big load of grass down to the puddle in a cart, emptied the grass into the water and stirred it around with long sticks. The children called it spinach. Gradually they began to lift up the slippery stuff and watch how the water ran off. Then they loaded the wet grass into the cart and took it over to the sand-pit, where they mixed it with sand and shaped it into a cake which they then proceeded to decorate with gravel and stones in neat circles, finally adding sticks for candles. The boy who had started the whole thing then instructed the others to sing "Happy Birthday" to him.

This example shows how important the availabity of different natural materials is and what a fine spirit of cooperation can develop among children when using materials which they can shape entirely in accordance with their own ideas.

Give chance a chance

In a natural setting such as a wood, there are chance events occurring all the time: a bird flies away, a leaf falls, there is a rustling noise. The shape of stems and stumps can suddenly seem to resemble something else and so fire a child's imagination. The woods can be changed; a branch can be bent down to make the rudder of a "boat", or twigs, leaves, fruit and berries can be gathered. The more one finds, the more one discovers. What playground today functions like this?

We have observed that it is often chance occurrences like the formation of a puddle that inspire children in their play. The bumpy or uneven or haphazard appeals to their fantasy and way of thinking. One could wish that playground planners would "give a chance to chance" - that is , provide an environment in which chance events were more likely to occur.

One way of "giving chance a chance" is to make the drainage system less perfect in some part of the playground. If one retains a cleft in a rock, for

example, **shallow** water can collect. Thick bushes and trees with hanging branches enable children to discover their own "secret" places. Asphalt can deliberately be made a little bumpy or pitted. At Viksjö, where the playground sneaks up into the woods in a wonderful way, water oozes down the rocks and forms a splendid gooey puddle in one corner of the playground. This is a resource that is used intensively by the children in their "cooking." In another area there is a muddy meadow which is a favorite place for bike-riding. It is interesting to ride on the slippery surface, skid, and see one's own tracks.

Obviously non-paved ground has real advantages for children. They can explore nature themselves and see what she provides. They can pick dandelions and other "weeds" and use them for baking cakes or playing store or, they can even fix up a bouquet for mother. If there is a little un-paved bit of ground, then there is also a chance to plant some flowers and vegetables.

A large boulder offers not only many different climbing experiences but also the chance to investigate the structure and irregularities of the stone and notice its temperature under different conditions, its color and so on. (Who can find a stone that is entirely grey?) We have seen an example of this at the park in Flysta in Spånga. There three boys, ages 7 - 10, were climbing on a huge stone. Each had his own special way of getting to the top, depending on the degree of difficulty he could manage. Moreover, each had found his own special "seat" which perfectly suited his bottom! The boys talked about some bigger boys who could scramble up a very difficult way, and they laughed at the observer who could only manage the simplest route of all.

When it comes to something so varied and exciting as a boulder, children can become downright experts regarding all the possibilities and difficulties offered. What type of fabricated play equipment arouses this kind of interest? (Did you know, by the way, that large rocks **turn** when they smell the aroma of pancakes?)

Sensory experiences

In childhood one is more open to sensory impressions than ever again in one's life. Smells, sensations of heat, softness and weight, and much, much more which every child needs the chance to experience form the basis of all of life's later sensations. To encounter again, as a grown-up, a particular smell or taste from childhood awakens memories from which we draw power and inspiration.

Seasonal changes

One aspect of variety which is important is how the playground changes with the change of seasons. It is questionable if children in many of our modern suburbs have the chance to get a basic understanding of the change of seasons. What they mostly see is worn-looking grass, twigs for bushes, supporting sticks and a tuft for trees, and asphalt. Seasonal change means burning-hot asphalt (summer), a grey period (autumn), snow and slush (winter), a grey period (spring) and a little cool rain now and then. Because of the way houses are built, there is often a constant wind in the area throughout the year. Experiencing the change of seasons is not only worthwhile and pleasurable in and of itself, it is also a basis for the development of a sense of time. Change as well as the permanency underlying change constitute ''sign-posts'' in the child's way of thinking which gradually come together as a unified concept of time. A tree, a branch, even an apple looks very different in the winter, spring, summer and autumn, but still it is basically the same. Grasping this paradox is a complicated intellectual process requiring the ability to follow and to recall a sequence of ideas, and to be aware of a variety of phenomena at the same time and put them in some relation to each other. This ability develops during childhood and forms the basis of our capacity to think logically.

The entire environment should be planned for children

A judicious planning of the residential environment as a whole would make many types of play equipment largely unnecessary. Much equipment is intended to provide chance for movement and exercise. Children need to be able to climb, balance, play ball, run around and chase each other, play hide-and-seek, get a view, and have a chance for both social contacts and solitude. Planning the entire residential area with children's needs in mind means that these and many other experiences can be provided in much greater variety than anything play equipment can offer. Suitable design of railings, curbstones, fences, planters, storage sheds, cellar steps, house walls and gardens can create many play opportunities. Moreover, careful attention to the original **resources** of an area, i. e. the rocky outcrops, stones, marshy land, dry shrubs, rotten stumps, bad drainage, muddy fields, overturned trees, remains of an old garden and so on would mean that the outdoor environment would **remain** rich and worth exploring.

A small children's enclosure with rocks and stumps, thickets, twigs, leaves and pine cones offers a whole world to be explored and used in play. A fence which instead of having sharp points is **meant** for balancing, a wall which can take having a ball hurled against it, a storage shed roof designed for climbing - all this would surely save a lot of play space. Instead areas could be planned for ball games, for riding bikes, for outings in nature.

In a residential area in Märsta, Ekilla, an old garden with apple trees, arbors, thick hedges and bushes with berries has been retained and become a fine resource for those living in the area. The roof of an old food cellar has been covered with masonite and is used for sliding, climbing and other play.

There could be nice places for sitting, fireplaces, areas where people can do their own planting, bushes with berries, trees with fruit, a workshop for doing repairs, bike trails, hidden corners for children filled with "junk" and boards, water play, animal enclosures and perhaps even a clubhouse. We must stop spending money on inflexible emergency solutions such as an excess of play equipment and pay attention instead to creating an environment which is suitable for creative activity on the part of both children and grown-ups.

19
A Place For All Ages

Admiring someone big and
helping someone little

Long and lanky and full of energy. Can we make the most of this?

Most of today's playgrounds are suited for children in a very limited age group. Sometimes one gets the feeling that those who plan play areas have a picture in their minds of **one** child of just the right age, about three or four, with not too great demands for excitement. But it is surely true that others both younger and older than the ideal child also need to find relaxation and stimulation in the outdoor environment. Besides contacts with grown-ups, children need to see and be together with older children who can serve as models. They also need chances to look after younger children in order to grasp the continuity in their own development and to have an outlet for their desire to take care of someone and not always be "worst" and smallest. The truly revolutionizing development which the child goes through on his way to becoming an adult is a hard job requiring constant adaptation to new situations and conditions. Other children who are themselves going through or have already gone through the same crisis are important in giving the child some perspective about himself and his own development. In his book *The Moral Judgment of the Child,* Jean Piaget speaks of the importance of the transmission of experience from children a little older to those a little younger. There is an enormous thrust towards socialization in the special relationship that develops between a young child and a playmate a little older whom he idolizes. No adult can fill this same function. The very fact that a friend has recently gone through the same development crisis as the child himself is now struggling with gives him a very special luster and authority. It is therefore disastrous to plan play areas close to home for small children **only** and expect children somewhat older to play elsewhere. It is tragic enough that residential areas in Sweden are as segregated as they are. The outdoor environment must be planned to counteract these tendencies as much as possible.

Our Yard

We know from earlier studies made in Sweden such as that of Sandel-Wohlin (1961) that children living in modern residential areas have a certain radius of movement within which they prefer to stay and do not willingly go beyond. This radius is more limited the younger the child. In the report on children's outdoor environment (SOU 1970) it is stated:

"The restrictions in radius of movement that have been observed are not to be interpreted as meaning that children can therefore be offered a clearly-defined area in which to move about." Unfortunately, however, there is a certain tendency among planners today to interpret research results in such a way that **only** the needs of quite small children are accommodated close to home and **only** the needs of bigger children are planned for in play areas a little further away. The Swedish Building Code of 1975 has had the effect of encouraging this trend; included in it is a statement that "the entrance area to a residential building should include a well-lit open surface large enough and suitably designed to meet the play needs of younger preschool children and the relaxation needs of grown-ups."

The trouble with this is that it is at least as important for older children as for younger ones to be able to play in their own yard. Bigger children can ride their bikes or walk to a larger soccer field for a game, but their own yard should offer them the chance to practice shooting goals or passing on a small scale. One's own yard, if it functions well, becomes a kind of **extended home**. We have noted several instances of how well local play areas can function with children of different ages playing together. At Bellman, for example, both big and little children enjoy using the high-jump equipment which the residents have obtained for the yard. The big children jump while the little ones look on. Later, when the big children have left, the younger children imitate what they saw or use the mat for rolling and bouncing around. At Nyby, younger children loved climbing on the structures in the carpentry area because they knew the older children had built them.

A playground intended for all ages has other advantages as well. The degree of difficulty of play can steadily increase in keeping with the individual child's need and rate of development. This provides the best possible conditions for growth since each child can on his own initiative try out something more difficult as soon as he has mastered an easier skill.

Can a child's center of security be shifted?

An understanding of how children function when it comes to radius of movement if taken too literally, can lead to segregation and categorization, as we have already pointed out. This is also mentioned in the Report on Children's Environment (Dahlén-Thiberg-Rönnmark: The child and the physical environment). The authors emphasize that one must keep in mind that observations regarding children's radius of movement have been made in modern residential areas and that little is known about how this principle functions in other types of areas. That the child's range of action expands in connection with his "greater ability to move about, larger play repertoire, increased self-assurance and decreased dependence on contact with the one taking care of him", (SOU 1970:1) cannot be doubted, however. The question is if the **entrance door** must be the center of the child's area of security. In a neighborhood experienced by the children as safe, and where the residents have a say in the design of the environment and an interest in all the children, then the radius of movement should be greater.

Play culture

Many playgrounds are segregated by age because the entire residential area is segregated. Very often an entire neighborhood is populated by young families at about the same time. All the children are thus of about the same age. Not only does this result in a very uneven burden on day-care centers and schools, it also involves great disadvantages for children as they have only others of the same age to play with. (For a fuller discussion of this point see Liljeström, R., 1973 and 1976). In the study of children's environments in different types of residential areas undertaken concurrently with our study (Dahlén, U., 1977) the observers note that in Viksjö in Järfälla outside Stockholm, an area of small single family houses, many of the games that they themselves had played as children seem to have disappeared. They mention certain variations of hopscotch, jump rope with all its different rhymes and rules, special ball games, different kinds of hide-and-seek, dancing and singing games, marbles, tug-of-war, games involving drawing with chalk on the pavement, and so on. It seems that at least in this particular residential area in Viksjö the transmission of a play culture from one generation of children to the next has not taken place. Interviews with mothers revealed, however that certain of these games, though not seen by the observers, were still played.

In our study we have observed that playing hopscotch and jumping rope live on, and that jumping twist (Chinese jump rope) is a game that has become popular since the time we were children. On the other hand, other games that we often played as children were **not** seen. (It is important to remember, however, that we made no observations after 4 p.m. so that we know nothing of the games played by older children in the evening.) That games die out in this way is a very serious consequence of our segregated residential patterns. As the study of Viksjö shows, children in single-family housing areas are hardly better off in this respect than other children.

Being too little

It is common in playgrounds that the youngest children who cannot reach, cannot manage, need to be watched closely all the time and often helped. The playground is not designed to promote their independence. As we stated when discussing the function of various types of equipment, many are either dangerous or else situated in such a way that small children cannot use them without constant supervision and help. Moreover, basic safety features such as a gate to the swing area or, in some cases, to the entire playground, are missing. The latter situation occurs at Stamgårdsparken. The planner states that the reason for this is to give an impression of openness. This openness has cost adults accompanying small children to the park a great deal of trouble because of the danger both from traffic in the nearby streets and from children riding their bikes at high speed right into the playground. It is very important to the development of children between the ages of one and three that their incipient independence and separation from parents is supported by the play environment. Among other things, the child must be able to increase his radius of action in relation to grown-up caring for him without risk of traffic or other injuries.

The grass is always greener
on the other side

One obstacle to having the alternation between moving away from and back to the adult function freely seems to lie in the very **concept of the playground.** It has been all too common at the places we have visited for adults constantly to bring children who have set out on an expedition of discovery back into the playground proper, preferably to the sand-pit. Since the environment in its entirety is not planned for play, adults stick to those enclosed places meant for play, where unfortunately many of the opportunities for a variety of experiences offered by the rest of the environment have been removed. For instance, the playground is often flat whereas the surroundings can be pleasantly hilly. Or the playground may contain only gravel while the area outside it may include soft grass, sharp rocks and slushy mud. Playgrounds often lack nooks and corners, while other areas may have building corners, spaces under balconies, hedges or large rocks for privacy or hiding.

In order to avoid a relationship between small child and mother at the playground that often results in the child becoming passive or inhibited, we must try to break up the concept of the playground and instead create **meeting places** for grown-ups and children. Rather than planning for play only in certain enclosed places, the entire residential area both indoors and out should be planned around the idea that children play wherever they happen to be.

Adult activities

With the exception of employed play leaders, we have very seldom observed adults taking part in childrens play or themselves engaging in some sort of adult activity outdoors. The little we have seen includes playing pat-a-cake with very small children or hide-and-seek or, at one playground, ping-pong. Once a mother stood holding a twist rope for her eight-year-old daughter who was waiting for her friend to come out.

Grown-ups often look as if playing pat-a-cake or pushing a swing was hopelessly boring. One baby-sitter sat for twenty minutes trying to read a magazine while a two-year-old boy nagged her to play pat-a-cake. She replied "You can play yourself" and continued reading. Now and then she sighed, gave up, and played a bit to the boy's great delight. When she got tired and stopped, he started nagging again. Finally he gave up and went over to the swings, leaving the baby-sitter to read in peace.

As playgrounds function today, the edge of the sand-pit or the swings is the usual meeting place for adults. The playground itself does not contribute to people getting to know each other. Rather, those who are already acquainted talk together intensively while the others concentrate on their own children. Contact with other adults often seems so important that people try in various ways to get their small children to play nearby, usually in the sand-pit, so they do not have to go away from the others. One mother expressed her weariness and irritation very openly. She refused for forty minutes to let her two-year-old daughter swing. She complained loudly to the other mothers "I hate the swings" and tried instead to get her daughter to sit in her stroller and "read" a book. When someone else went over to the swings, she gave in and pushed her daughter a short while before going home.

That grown-ups are so bored at playgrounds surely has a very negative effect on children's play. A bored grown-up is no inspiring model for a child. Besides giving adults a chance to engage in some stimulating activity, it is good if play equipment is designed so that it can be used without help even by young children. Not only does this promote the child's independence, it also frees adults from doing something they consider very boring.

The adult world as inspiration for play

What adults do has great significance as a source of inspiration for children's play, as we have observed again and again. At Hallonbergen play park, for example, it was possible one day to smell asphalt and hear the talk of some workmen busy near by. This inspired three boys, 5 - 7 years' old, to begin making asphalt from sand and water and then taking this in wagons over to a flower bed which was surrounded by an edge of stone. There they proceeded to add an extra border of "asphalt mortar." In the sand-pit at Nyby children played at being workmen after watching an excavation project going on nearby. Children in a single-family housing area in Viksjö built houses of sand and made remarks like "the toilet doesn't work", "tell us if the doors or windows are no good" and so on. In one of the playhouses at Hallonbergen some 5 - 7-year-old girls played with two younger children and revealed how they perceived a day in the life of a mother with small children. In rapid succession their "children" were commanded, "Now you are to eat, now go to sleep, now get dressed, now we'll read a story" and "later you can eat again."

Lack of experience of the adult world is reflected in make-believe and role play, which is often one-sided.

On Resarö wells are drilled in many places. This is reflected in children's play. "We must drill for water before we can start building."

Playing one's way into the adult world

Children have the opportunity in their play to incorporate all sorts of adult roles as an aspect of their own personality. But for symbolic play to develop it is necessary that they have access to adult models, and this is precisely what children in today's society all too often lack in their everyday world. Those adults they come in contact with are mostly their own parents and those who look after them while their parents are working.

What children very seldom have a chance to observe are friendships between adults or solidarity and cooperation in work situations. Nor do children have a chance to observe the hard competition, struggle and stress which today's working life involves, except in so far as it makes their parents irritable and tired. They never see the whole picture, cannot understand why things happen, and have a hard time preparing for life as an adult. Since the function of symbolic play is to "melt down" and incorporate all the impressions which the child absorbs, play gets stuck in "idle" if the child is not exposed to a variety of roles and models.

Symbolic play suffers doubly. Because of the sterility of the child's total environment, the lack of materials for creating with, the lack of chances to take part in productive adult life, the separation from natural processes and the lack of a perspective both forward and backward, even the content of play becomes meager and sterile. **Reality nourishes play.** It is real life that continually serves as the stimulus to play. The child growing up under favorable conditions strives to grasp and understand everything; the more the child has absorbed in the way of experience, the more unexplored elements pile up which insist on being investigated. In this way, step by step, the child works his way out of his egocentric world. If the environment does not provide him these opportunities, much material remains unprocessed and perhaps never is fully incorporated into the personality. Situations that the individual first encounters as an adult are often much more difficult to absorb. The more limited his experiences as a child, the more limited are his options concerning both and adult role and a profession.

Being too big - and too little

The most neglected age group of all is unquestionably the somewhat older child, from 7 - 15 years. At many of the playgrounds we visited there have been no children of this age present at all, while at other places they have shown up only sporadically. Still, we have seen examples of how it is possible to keep even these children occupied and involved. Here follows a description of some of the activities that we have found children of this age eager to engage in.

Meeting peers

At all the playgrounds we visited, contacts with other children have been very much in the center of what older children do. This contact has taken different forms at different places, depending largely on what activities were available. It is very common at unsupervised playgrounds for children 7 - 10 to gather, hang or climb on some piece of equipment or around the swings and talk, giggle or just be together. Equipment often functions as a place to meet and decide what to do next. The particular design of the equipment seems to have extremely little relevance for this purpose, as it is used not for play but for socializing.

Moving around

Riding bikes around somewhat aimlessly is very common. Children ride from one yard to another, often in a gang. Biking also serves as a form of competition or a way to train balance. It is a popular activity both in apartment and single-family housing areas. It is also very common for older children to ride their bikes to a playground lying at some little distance from home.

Bike riding presents a problem at many playgrounds and, because of risk to small children, is usually forbidden. But it is very difficult to get children to observe this rule, especially since so many playgrounds are largely asphalt. Special bike tracks and the availability of large tricycles, scooters and pedal cars are good approaches to trying to solve the problem.

Besides bike riding, the activities which predominate among children of this age at unsupervised playgrounds include soccer and ground hockey for the boys and jumping rope, twist, and hopscotch for the girls. Sometimes boys and girls play tag or hide-and-seek together, and at a few playgrounds mixed groups have used the high-jump equipment or played ball. The amount girls and boys play together has varied considerably from one place to another.

Building something

At supervised playgrounds there has naturally been a greater variety of activities offered. Where available, building materials and tools appeal very much to 7 - 12-year-olds. Carpentry provides a chance for creative construction, for cooperation, and for learning. Moreover through this activity children often come in close contact with the play leader. Building activity has different characteristics at different stages. At the beginning planning and construction of houses is central. Gradually as more and more huts and other structures are completed, the carpentry corner becomes a place to play tag or just be together with others. Such an area requires more supervision than other play areas. Vandalism is a problem, as is the risk of fire and the fact that people (often adults!) steal lumber. These problems are not easy to solve. Still, it is a well-documented fact that a properly supervised carpentry area offers such great advantages to children that it is well worth the necessary investment of money and energy. (See Mejer, E., 1970) Children have a need to create and change things. Without some chance to satisfy this need constructively, the creative urge finds an outlet in destruction instead.

Taking responsibility for an animal

Another activity which is very attractive to older children is the care and feeding of animals. Many children today have no chance to come into contact with animals in their normal environment. Animals give them a chance to show affection and tenderness. They provide something to do and someone to take care of. In addition, children learn a great deal about what animals can eat, how to keep them and the places they live in clean, and so on. Taking responsibility for an animal can be a very important experience for a child.

Being useful

Older children are often very glad to have the chance to help with an adult job. One such opportunity is growing things. Gardening gives the child a chance to follow the development from seed to flower or ripe fruit. It is an exciting process, and one which involves much learning. To understand the permanent in the changing - that this flower I now hold in my hand comes from the seed I planted before - is a complicated intellectual process. Gardening also offers concrete knowledge about the relationship of earth, air and water, how chlorophyll is formed and how we must take care of all growing things since we cannot survive without them.

Rule games

Even at supervised play parks, soccer and ground hockey are common. Also popular are boccie, tennis,. These games are often played by girls and boys together. Our impression is that at supervised playgrounds, because of the wider range of activities offered, boys and girls play together more often than at unsupervised playgrounds. But even at supervised playgrounds they often play separately.

Another activity which is very popular among older children is the high-jump. Ping-pong was played rarely outdoors, but more often inside. Stockholm's park department has several types of materials which have maintained their popularity through the years, such as stilts and chests of building blocks. Games are also popular and much used. They offer a nice chance for a quiet chat with the play leaders.

Water

Something which attracts all children, including older ones, is water. The water play at Fisksätra and Upplands-Väsby has proved to be of great interest to children up to about the age of thirteen. At Fisksätra older children sailed balls of paper, built dams or helped the staff clean out the pool. At Upplands Väsby they splashed and bathed uninhibitedly, sometimes with clothes on, in the canal. A hydrant, a water tap or a hose is enough to stimulate all kinds of games.

Someone who has time

Many of the supervised playgrounds we visited function as a sort of after-school center or extended home. Children ages 7 - 10 still have a strong need for **continuous** contact with adults. The demands put on them in school to sit still, listen, do what the teacher says, and find their place among a group of children are often difficult to manage. It is therefore extremely important that children have somewhere near home to go after school where they feel welcome and where there are grown-ups they know well. Those playgrounds which function best in this respect are supervised playgrounds lying quite close to a residential area. At such places we have noted that contact with the staff has meant a great deal to older children. These contacts are often relaxed, without demands. At Haren on Söder in Stockholm the children usually sit and play games with the leader and talk. Adults living in the area also stop by and exchange a few words with the personnel. At Upplands-Väsby the staff plays and jokes with the children, has a snack together with them and starts up some game now and then. What is most important for the children's well-being is probably that someone they know is around, someone who has time to listen to them.

Meeting places in the residential area.

In order to develop and gain an understanding of adult life, children must not be cut off from adult places of work and occupations, as happens all too often today. To some degree it is possible to compensate for this if at least in their free time children and grown-ups have a reason to be together and a place where it is natural for people of all ages to congregate.

One idea worth considering is to plan not for separate playgrounds but instead for natural meeting places and some type of leisure center with opportunities for both indoor and outdoor activities. Those meeting places that exist today include the laundry rooms, corner grocery, elevator, and -for those with small children - edge of the sand-pit. It would be desirable through careful planning to increase the number of such places, not least in areas with row-houses or single-family houses. By arranging outdoor activities for both children and adults such as small gardens, pleasure boat harbors, minigolf, beautiful paths for walking, jogging and skiiing tracks, tennis, soccer, volleyball, complemented with public places such as a cafeteria, hobby room, workshop, or car wash, it would be possible to increase significantly the chances for residents of an area to meet each other.

We have previously pointed to Upplands-Väsby as an example of an attempt to plan for the needs of all age groups. Also in Husby, a newly developed suburb of Stockholm, there has been an effort to satisfy the needs of adults by placing a neighborhood activity center next to the playground. Here there is a cafeteria with cheap prices and a large room used for playing ping-pong, dancing or viewing performances by visiting theater groups. The building contains several other rooms where courses of all kinds are held both day and evening for children, young people and adults.

Music bridges the generation gap.

20
Remember

If we are to minimize the inadequacies of our playgrounds, we must keep in mind the following:

- Provide chances for children of all ages to find an outlet for their need to move about in a meaningful context.
- Create the right conditions for role play and make-believe.
- Give children a chance to learn something about nature and natural processes.
- Provide children the opportunity for contact with others of the same age and frame of mind so they can get a perspective on themselves.
- Provide children the opportunity for contact with younger and older children so they can get a sense of the continuity of their own development.
- Make it possible for children to take part in the everyday adult world.
- Make it possible for adults to engage in meaningful outdoor activities. This must be based on increased influence in both planning and management on the part of those who **live** in the area.
- Stop thinking in terms of playgrounds. Instead, plan the entire environment for play and activity and try to create natural meeting places in the residential area!

How can these things be accomplished? And what are the special interests that work against the needs of children being satisfied?

APPENDIX 1

Unsupervised playgrounds

Ranking of fixed play equipment and surfaces in order of average frequency of use, expressed in per cent.

Faltoversten

(used 75 - 80 % of the time)

Item	%
ASPHALT	44.9
two Swings	12.7
GRAVEL	11.6
	8.3

(used 20 - 25 % of the time)

Item	%
sand-pit	6.3
small combination e.g. with slide	5.2
large climbing frame with net	4.6
DRY POOL	4.1
ping-pong table	0.8
round house without roof	0.0

Brandbergen

(used 75 - 80 % of the time)

Item	%
ASPHALT PATHS	38.0
sand-pits	20.3
swings	12.9
GRASS WITH HILL	5.5

(used 20 - 25 % of the time)

Item	%
GRASS BETW SAND-PITS	5.5
two slides on asphalt terraces	4.8
FLOWER BEDS	3.5
carousel with wheel	2.3
cement boat	1.8
two houses without roof	1.4
fence maze	1.2
backboard	1.2
stumps	1.1
balance beams	0.9
wooden bar	0.2
angled	0.2
climbing tree	0.0
	0.0

Tingvalla

(used 75 - 80 % of the time)

Item	%
ASPHALT	26.0
GRASS	12.0
SAND-PIT	12.0
SAND AROUND EQ	11.3
high climbing frame w tower, net, ropes, rope ladder	7.5
small combination e.g. with slide	7.0

(used 20 - 25 % of the time)

Item	%
BENCHES, CARPET-BEATING RACK, FLOWER BED,	5.5
STAIRS	4.0
large playhouse backboard, goal	3.5
plastic tower	2.8
swings	2.4
aerial ropeway (only in spring)	1.6
timber house	1.2
store front	0.9
look-out tower	0.6
small house, roof	0.2
ping-pong table	0.2

Bellman

(used 75 - 80 % of the time)

Item	%
sand-pit	23.5
GRASS	17.0
ASLPHALT	15.8
SAND AROUND EQ	12.9
wide slide on grass slope	9.5

(used 20 - 25 % of the time)

Item	%
swings	5.0
tractor tire swing	4.0
SHRUBS,	3.5
CLIMBING TREE	1.6
STAIRS, CARPET RACK, ENTRIES	1.2
steel bar	1.0
climbing tree	0.1

Stamgardsparken

(used 75 - 80 % of the time)

Item	%
ASPHALT	21.9
Sand-pit	21.5
SOCCER FIELD	15.1
Swings	11.2
comb climbing house with slide	7.5

(used 20 - 25 % of the time)

Item	%
WOOD CHIPS rain hut w net	5.4
	5.4
BENCHES	4.8
rocking horses	4.5
GRAVEL	1.6
PERGOLA	0.8
DRINKING FOUNTAIN	0.5

These have been used 75 - 80 % of the time

These have been used 20 - 25 % of the time

APPENDIX 2

Supervised playgrounds
Ranking of fixed play equipment and surfaces in order of average frequency of use, expressed in per cent

Fisksatra

These have been used 75 - 80 % of the time

Equipment / surface	%
ASPHALT	26.3
CARPENTRY CORNER	11.9
GRASS	8.3
SAND AROUND SWINGS	7.7
narrow, long and short, wide slide on wooded slope	7.4

These have been used 20 - 25 % of the time

Equipment / surface	%
look-out tower	6.2
tractor-tire swing, vertical tire	3.0
NATURAL TERRAIN	3.0
BIKE PIT	2.9
swings	2.3
RAIN ROOF	2.3
playhouse (only available part of the spring)	1.0
three houses w roof	1.8
aerial ropeway	1.5
STONE MAZE	1.4
ping-pong table	0.8
fire-place	0.2
	0.2

Orminge

Equipment / surface	%
comb climbing frame w slide hammock	26.5
sand-pit	16.8
ASPHALT	14.8
CARPENTRY CORNER	6.7
train, snail, tent and mushroom house	6.2
WOODS, ROCKS, HILLS	5.4
aerial ropeway	5.1
GRAVEL	5.0
VERANDA	3.6
adventure park	2.8
narrow slide on grass slope	2.4
GRASS	2.3
ping-pong table	2.3
swings	1.0
TABLE AND BENCH	0.6

Nyby

Equipment / surface	%
sand-pit	21.2
DRY POOL	21.1
swings	12.0
CARPENTRY CORNER	10.2
GRASS	9.8
SAND AROUND EQ	7.1
plastic modules	4.1
two short, narrow slides on grass hill	3.5
climbing house w steps	1.9
large play house	1.9
three small houses w roof	1.5
rocking horses	1.4
BENCHES, BIKE RACK, ENTRY	1.4
large climbing frame w ropes, net, rope ladder	1.3
balance beams	1.3
fixed wood pigs	0.1

Hallonbergen

Equipment / surface	%
ASPHALT FIELD	26.5
sand-pit	15.3
FOOTBALL FIELD	11.8
GRAVEL FIELD	8.4
comb. climbing frame w slide	5.8
ASPHALT PATHS	6.4
two chests of blocks	4.4
two wide slides of different lengths anchored in rock	3.6
swings	3.0
PLACE WITH WIND SHELTER, BENCHES AND TABLES	3.0
playhouse in shed x	
bike carousel	2.2
aerial rope way x	2.2
SAND UNDER EQ	2.2
rain shelter without net	1.4
ping-pong table	1.3
w roof	1.1
"STORY PLACE"	0.1

Upplands-Vasby

Equipment / surface	%
ASPHALT	50.5
GRASS	10.2
large slide and two slides on slope	9.4
ANIMAL ENCLOSURE	8.7
WOODS AND ROCKS	6.1
house at water play	4.7
SAND AROUND EQ	4.4
aerial ropeway	4.4
suspension bridge	1.5
swings	0.9
large climbing frame w ropes, net, rope ladder	0.8
bridges at shower	0.4
wooden bar	0.3
three different towers	0.2
climbing frame w net (NT 150)	0.1
balance beams in sand, woods	0.0

X = closed/broken most of the time

APPENDIX 3

SUMMARY OF RESULTS OF INVESTIGATION INTO THE FUNCTIONAL VALUE OF PLAYGROUND EQUIPMENT

Equipment for exercise

Equipment for exercise—simple function:
1 Balancing equipment (balance beams, low climbing and balancing equipment, shipwreck)
2 Climbing frames of wood (with and without rope ladders, rope lines and nets)
3 Climbing frames of steel
4 Vaulting equipment
5 Ball and climbing planks (walls with marked goal posts and with holes)

Equipment for exercise combined with sensory experience— speed, spinning and dizziness:
6 Swings (traditional swings and tractor-tire swings)
7 Rocking-horse
8 Spinning seesaw (movable equipment)
9 Suspension bridge
10 Aerial ropeway
11 Carousel
12 Slide

Equipment for exercise—combined functions. Movement in combination with other factors such as rule-games, symbol-games and sensory experience:

13 Small combination equipment
14 Large combination equipment
15 Games

Equipment with which to pretend, create and construct

Static representational equipment:

16 Animals (fixed and movable)
17 Boats
18 Sculptures (plastic and metal)
19 Tree trunks

Room-creating equipment:

20 Small huts (with and without roofs)
21 Screens (commercial screens)
22 Towers (wood and plastic)
23 Playhouses (with steps and flat roof, storage module and traditional playhouse)
24 Protective wind and rain cover

Constructive materials

25 Building sets (boxes)
26 Sand boxes (pits)

Equipment for exercise—simple function:

Balancing equipment

Balancing beams and ropes were used 27 of 3790 possible minutes, or 0.07% of the time. (By possible minutes we mean the time we have observed a single child, that is to say during the one hour of an observation period. When we indicate that we have not seen a certain piece of equipment used at all, this means neither during the systematic observation nor during the whole visit at the playground.)

Balancing on manufactured beams was equally rare among all age groups. However, observations indicate that children of all ages enjoy balancing, but that they would rather use for this purpose fences, walls, curbs, cahlk lines, stones and stumps. Since it is a part of this form of play to **choose** a place that is exciting and reasonably difficult to balance upon, it is a fundamental error to place special equipment for this purpose on the playground. The degree of difficulty of such equipment is too fixed to offer, in the long run, a challenge to play.

Low climbing frames and balancing equipment were used during 11 of 965 minutes, or 1.15% of the time.

Much of the low climbing and balancing equipment such as climbing planks, "the cross" and jungle-gyms have not been used at all either in the spring or fall. This equipment lacks any meaningful function. The need for small children for balancing and climbing play is best served by retaining hills, stones and stumps and by designing the whole environment so as to provide broad and varied experiences.

The revolving barrel was used 0 minutes of 169.

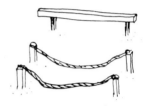

This piece of equipment may be viewed as a cynical example of how children are regarded as a kind of white mice who must be kept occupied with play machines. This equipment totally lacks excitement and is also dangerous. Children can easily fall and knock out their teeth. Stop producing it. Children need space to run in, not treadmills.

The "shipwreck" was used 50 of 365 minutes, or 13% of the time.

The so-called ladder of the shipwreck is used by children primarily as a slide, for want of anything better, although it was intended that they should run over it. The result is torn clothes. It is used largely by smaller children, but never as the unit intended. Smaller children are unable to grasp this equipment as a single unit. Older children who are able to grasp the idea of a system of equipment find its separate parts far too easy to cope with and hardly inspiring to new games. That which is used most is the sand under the equipment and the water that gathers there. A better alternative would be to supply the playground with lose stumps, planks etc., so that the children could make their own "shipwreck".

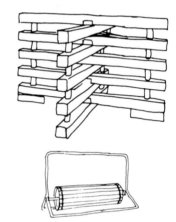

Adventure equipment was used 45 of 1660 minutes, or 3% of the time.

The adventure equipment is off to one side and competes with similar equipment on the playground. The older children use the beams, ropes, net, tunnel, tower and slide as a single unit.

They practice moving through it in different ways and even make up rules for the game. In the majority of cases a number of children play together. The smaller children are most attracted to the slide and tunnel. They use only certain parts. Placement on uneven land improves the climbing and balancing potential provided by nature. The wide range in the degree of difficulty among the various parts of the shipwreck allows children, at their own tempo, to increase the degree of difficulty in their activity.

Climbing frames of wood

The climbing tree was used 2 minutes of 1140, or 0.2% of the time.

This equipment has a limited function. Its construction is such that children under five can hardly climb it. Its low height and lack of potential variation also make it unappealing to older children. With its purely climbing function this equipment is a typical example of faulty thinking. Children of the age this type of equipment is intended for need stimulation for their imagination and rule-games, which this equipment does not give. Provide children with real trees to climb, large apple and pear trees, for instance!

The climbing frame "Stockholm" was used 25 minutes of 2020 possible, or 1.3% of the time.

This equipment has a low use frequency and is rather difficult for children between four and seven. Children practice different ways of getting through and up in the climbing frame. They hang by their legs and practice standing on top without holding on. Children under three amused themselves by climbing through the "gangways" at ground level. Children over seven sit on top of the equipment and talk. One advantage of this equipment is that the climbing bars are so close together that there is always

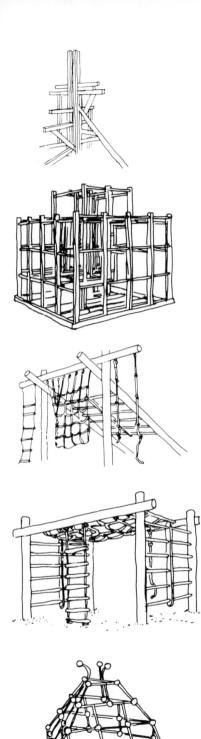

something to hold onto. Lose bits of cloth, ropes, bits of planks, paper cartons enhance its use.

Climbing frame with rope, net and rope ladders: frame with two vertical and two angled legs was used 33 of 2305 minutes, or 1.4% of the time.

Children of approximately five years and up can cope with this equipment. Smaller children swing on the rope ladders or hang on the rope. The ropes are often tied together to serve as a swing, which is frequently unsatisfactory and thus ordinary swings are preferred. The leaning ladder bars present a danger to smaller children since they can easily climb them but are unable to see the danger of falling down between them. This, as well as other similar leaning ladders, creates an element of stress at the playground, since adults must constantly stop the smaller children from using them.

Frames with four legs and ropes or nets for a roof were used 85 minutes of 4630 possible, or 1.8% of the time.

Used little by all ages. The smaller children can only use the ropes and rope ladder. The children try to use them as swings but soon stop since the ropes do not provide as much speed or relaxation as an ordinary swing. From about the age of five the ladder and net are used. The older children use the net to lie in and rest, look about and talk. Occasionally the equipment was used to play tag and in trying to find different ways of crawling through the net. At one playground the equipment was used as a football goal. On one occasion at another playground the net broke and children became actively engaged in trying to creep through the hole.

Climbing frames of steel

Steel climbing frames were used 55 minutes of a possible 1355, or 4% of the time.

This relative high frequency of use was in a park to which children were taken by adults. It would appear that play equipment does not lose its "newness" as quickly in distant parks as it does in neighborhood playgrounds.

Children have used this equipment for very brief periods. Only in rare cases have they remained more than ten minutes. On these occasions the equipment was complemented with loose planks and "junk". Steel climbing frames are often low and hardly exciting for older children. Smaller children who could experience the height as exciting can seldom climb them because the distance between the bars is too great. Usually there is no alternative "easy way" for the smaller children to climb. Certain frames in which one or more of the bars is free standing, as it were, may be used as a pole-vault. Sometimes the frame may function as a "room structure" so that the children may sit under it and play. Pieces of cloth, planks, boxes and buckets used as supplementary materials increase the number of pretend-games around a frame. This equipment requires a soft floor or base. Unfortunately many of these frames are found on hard gravel, which is obviously unsuitable.

Vault bars

Vaulting equipment of wood was used 7 of 2830 minutes, or 0.24% of the time.

Vaulting equipment of wood is among the least-used type of equipment. Wood must be of too robust a dimension for children's hands to grasp. In addition there is the danger of slivers of impregnated wood, which, according to our information, are more dangerous than ordinary slivers since the body is not able to break them down.

Vaulting equipment of steel was used 128 of 4410 minutes, or 3.10% of the time on the average. It is apparent that vaulting equipment is used a great deal at some playgrounds and not at all at others. This depends on how centrally placed the equipment is and on what other alternatives are available. Children from about five years and up vault, hang by their legs and swing in pairs. The social play or sense of togetherness is important. Comparisons are made between what tricks can be performed. It contributes to exercise in which the child lifts its own weight, which is important, according to gymnastic experts. Higher bars attract older children too. A box as an accessory allows smaller children to reach the bar and perform simple exercises such as hanging by the arms.

Ball and climbing wall

Ball walls with marked goal posts were used 64 of 4090 minutes, or 1.55% of the time. At **one** playground during the autumn a ball wall was used 10% of the time.

Ball planks with goal posts marked on them were used to bounce a ball, kick a football against and to practice tennis, especially by children of seven years and up. The smaller children used the climbing bars to climb the backside of the wall, where children as young as two-years old could climb. At a number of playgrounds ball walls have not been used at all and children bounced balls instead against the walls of buildings, ventilation funnels, or they have chosen to use goal posts or nets for playing ball. They have also used stones or their jackets to mark goal posts. The low height of ball walls, as compared with building walls, and the fact that the ball does not go **in** the goal are clearly disadvantages. Varied ground, decent sized walls for bouncing balls, and goal posts and nets are preferable to ball planks.

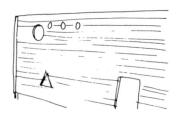

Ball planks with holes were used 4 minutes of 1135, or 0.20% of the time.

When ball planks are too low and, in addition, often do not go all the way to the ground, they fail to serve their purpose. Using the holes to play peek-a-boo, or throwing a ball through the holes has occurred rarely. Peek-a-boo has a much more heightened effect when indulged through the wall of a hut, for instance, where the contrast between light and darkness enhances the excitement.

Equipment for exercise combined with sensory experience—speed, spinning around and dizziness:
Swings

Traditional swings were used 925 of 16930 minutes, or 5.4% of the time. At supervised playgrounds the average was 3-4%, whereas children at unsupervised playgrounds used the swings 10-12% of the time. The swings were used less if the children had access to alternatives such as loose materials,

building games etc. Frequency in the use of swings varied considerably in relation to the availability of alternatives and the placement of the swings. The swings were used by children of all ages but in different ways. For the younger children swinging provides a pleasurable sensation, while also giving a sense of security; the children hum and enjoy the rhythmical motion. For children over three swinging presents a challenge to produce the speed themselves, to spin and twist and push each other and to long-jump from the swing. By the age of five, however, the social function of the swings becomes more predominate. For children of school age the swings are almost exclusively a place to meet, to sit and talk, to tease each other, or to sing and rest while they decide what they shall do next.

Tire swings appear more to stimulate playing together than straight swings of wood, plastic or cloth fabric. Wooden swings are painful to be hit in the head with and fabric swings squeeze the children uncomfortably and easily turn over. Baby swings in which a year-old child may be safely placed are a must among playground swings, since children greatly enjoy swinging, and it is a serious stress factor for adults if the swings are unsafe.

To keep children from running in under the swings, an area should be fenced off five meters in front and five meters behind the swings. There should be sand under the swings, of uniform grain, which cannot be used for building games.

Tractor-tire swings were used 110 of 3890 minutes, or 2.8% of the time.

This equipment was not used by children under three years old, despite the fact that the tire is big enough for an adult and child to swing together. Because the equipment is heavy, a number of children often helped push to speed up the swing. It happnes often that children of different ages swing together; the smaller children merely sit and hold on while the older children work hard to gain speed. The tractor-tire swing will not gain the same height and speed as an ordinary swing, but this is offset by the extra tingling sensation enjoyed on this type of swing, caused by the weight of the tire. Ordinary swings attracted the children at least as often as the tire swings and sometimes more often. The heavey tractor tires encourage cooperation, which is true also of the ordinary tire swings, but the disadvantage is that a child cannot swing by himself if he wishes to do so.

Because the tractor tire is heavy there is always the risk that it will fall and injure smaller children. Therefore tractor-tire swings should be hung or placed separate from the other swings.

Rocking-horses were used 110 minutes of 2825, or 3.7% of the time.

This equipment appealed primarily to smaller children. Children under three are not always able themselves to start the rocking-horse but are highly attracted to the idea of climbing up on it by themselves. Children of this age frequently stop rocking so as to climb off and on the rocking-horse again. From about three years of age the rocking varies and the social element becomes stronger. The children imitate each other, sit backwards and do "tricks". Children over five use the equipment more in passing, as it were. They stand on the rocking-horse and do tricks, play circus etc. Rocking-horses are more appealing when placed in groups along with other materials such as ropes, pails and pieces of cloth to help stimulate the imagination. Certain older models are dangerous since children can catch or jam their feet in them.

Spinning seesaw

Spinning seesaw, "loose" equipment was used 80 minutes of 4265, or 1.8% of the time. Use frequency varied from 0.5 to 5.5% of the time.

This equipment was used by children of all ages. The smallest children need an adult to teeter with them and occasionally someone to hold them. From about the age of three children can manage to teeter themselves without help from adults, and they then begin to discover that they can "cooperate in the teeter-tottering. The seesaw encourages experimentation with gravity and "pretend" games such as horseback riding, while the older children may indulge in balancing exercises by seesawing standing up and placing counter weights on the seesaw. The combination of vertical and sideward motion increases the excitement. The construction of the equipment discourages its use as a carousel, which is a good thing considering the giddness and mobbing often associated with carousels.

Suspension bridge

Suspension bridge, the high model, was only observed in **one** playground and was used 25 minutes of 1635, or 1.4% of the time.

The high type of suspension bridge is suitable only for children from five or six and up. Supervision by adults is essential if younger children use it. The danger is primarily that children with varying balancing ability will run and jump on the suspension bridge and that younger, weaker children may fall or be knocked off it. The suspension bridge can present a challenge for the older children by testing their ability to climb up on it, run along it, swing on it and remain there without falling off. The suspension bridge should span a creek, ditch or some other depression in the ground, or span the distance between two mounds. It is important that the suspension bridge be equipped so that even the smaller children have something to hold onto.

Aerial ropeway

The aerial ropeway was used 190 minutes of 3825, or an average of 3.35% of the time. Frequency of use varied greatly: between 1 to 2% at three playgrounds and 5% of the time at two playgrounds.

The aerial ropeways were often non-functional, which naturally influenced the frequency of use. Children of five years and up manage very well on the aerial ropeway, but even smaller children can cope with it with the help of an adult. This necessitates the ropeway being equipped with a tire in which the children can sit. The aerial ropeway encourages play in which the children may test the potential of their own bodies and their bravery. They travel backwards, hang by their stomachs and stand or sit on top of the tire. The children experiment with different starting speeds and heights. They have fantasized about where they were going and have also made rules about how they should travel down the ropeway. The ropeway encourages cooperation: the children help each other into the tire, they retrieve the tire for each other. They discuss whose turn it is and the proper technique for riding down the rope. If the aerial ropeway is to function in the manner described above, it must be long and stretched down a natural slope. A serious disadvantage to the aerial ropeway is that it is easily damaged.

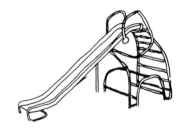

Carousels

Carousels, small carousels with a steering wheel and cycle carousels, were used 15 of 1235 minutes, or 1.2% of the time.

Sporadically this equipment appeals to children of all ages, but primarily to children under five. The cycle carousel was used in such a way that children under three rode on it, while children from three to five years old cycled round and round. It happened occasionally that children pretended to be "mechanics" or that they pretended to travel some place. There was also a tendency to mobbing, and children sometimes deserted their companions. The steering-wheel carousel too was used mostly by smaller children. They stamped on the steel platform, climbed on the steering wheel and lay on their stomachs to feel the sand as they spun around. The function of the carousel was served equally well by ordinary tire swings. Cycling or pushing each other about may be done just as well or better on tricycles. We know from experience that carousels, especially where mixed age groups are involved, can bring about mobbing. Riding the carousel makes children giddy, and many models are dangerous in that children may be pinched or injured. Therefore the carousel is unnecessary equipment.

Slides

Slides with steps or ladder were used 50 of 1720 minutes, of which 40 minutes was in **one** playground. The average frequency in the other playgrounds was 0.7%, and in the extreme case 9.9%. Slides anchored on a slope were used 490 of 8740 minutes, or 6.8% of the time. The frequency of use varied between 3.5 and 10.5%, with one exception. This latter concerned two slides anchored to an artificial asphalt hill. These slides were used 0.47% of the time and obviously functioned as badly as a slide with ladder, as far as the children were concerned.

It has been shown that there is a marked difference in the function of slides with ladders and those anchored to a slope. The latter type of slide is used by children from one-year-old up to 10 or 12. Particularly if the slope is fitted with railroad ties, for then even the smaller children can climb to the top of the slide again at their own pace without being pushed aside or hindering the older ones. They may also change their mind if they like without slowing down the others. The narrow slides with steps or ladders are too difficult for smaller children to climb and offer too little excitement for the older children that can climb the steps easily. It has also been shown that children generally go down the slides with ladders alone, whereas on slides placed on sloping ground they will often slide down together, two or three at a time, thus intensifying their pleasure through cooperative play. Narrow anchored slides are preferable for smaller children. They can support themselves by hanging onto the sides of the slide and also regulate their speed themselves. From the age of three and up to 10 and 12 broader slides are fine.

The slide is a source of play and experiments with speed, friction, gravity, sound, and gives experience of height and shifting perspective. The children test various ways of going down and **up** the slide. They release various objects of different weights and friction down the slide. They slide down on quilts, cardboard, pieces of planking, sand, gravel and the seat of their pants. By allowing their bodies to fall or slide under safe conditions the children learn to deal with their inherent fear of bodily injury. The slide is often the source of contact between children, both unconscious physical contact and social contact through organized games with rules and symbols. The children play tag or follow-the-leader or pretend they are a train puffing down the slide.

It is clearly an advantage if the slide is placed on natural ground where pine-cones, sticks, stones and gravel are available to enhance their sliding play. Pieces of cloth, corrugated cardboard and pieces of planking also enhance the pleasure of their play. Slides for smaller children should be placed in areas that are pleasant for adults too. It is very important that the slides are not placed where they present a barrier to children's winter play, such as sledding and skiing.

Equipment for exercise—combined functions: (Movement in combination with other factors such as rule-games, symbol-games and sensory experience.)

Small combination equipment

Big playhouse with climbing bars and sheet-metal slide was used 210 of 4285 minutes, or 5.25% of the time. Top playhouse with masonite slide was used 80 minutes of 1540, or an average of 4% of the time.

The result for the big playhouse was uniform and clear-cut, while the use frequency of the top playhouse varied between 0 and 12.6%. This higher use frequence was noted at Faltaversten where two playhouses were placed next to each other, which enabled the older boys to use them while playing tag.

The design of the big playhouse makes it suitable equipment for smaller children, those from 1 to 3 years old. The climbing bars provide an opportunity to train under safe circumstances. The area under the roof gives a certain seclusion but also makes it possible for the adults to see what is happening there. The top playhouse is, on the other hand, less suitable for smaller children. To get up to the top of the playhouse requires a certain length of legs if a child is to run up to the top. This equipment therefore appeals mostly to older children, although children of three or four can manage it. Both these types of equipment are used by children **up to** school age (seven in Sweden). The children use them for exercise play and pretend-games such as playing family and baking etc. and in certain cases for rule-games such as tag.

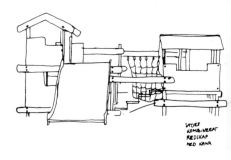

STORT
KOMBINERAT
REDSKAP
MED KANA

The playhouse with climbing tower and slide was used 55 minutes of 625, or 8.95% of the time. The playhouse of this type is at a playground where there is **little** fixed equipment but lots of lose materials such as ropes, tires, tarpaulin, sawhorses, stumps, sticks, inner-tubes, buckets etc. The equipment has therefore functioned for intense symbolic games with role-playing. It has functioned as a ship, a fort, and a riding school, and the children have experimented with gravity by dropping various objects down through the tower and by lifting other objects on ropes. Since the slide is constructed as a playhouse it also appeals to the smallest children.

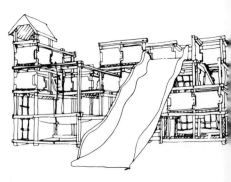

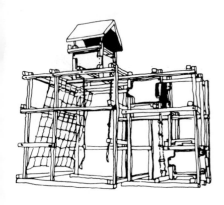

Small climbing-slide and playhouse combined was used 110 minutes of 1655, or 6.10% of the time.

This equipment was used primarily by children of pre-school age. From a fairly early age children can use this equipment to climb, slide and jump from various heights. When placed in isolation and with buckets, discarded dishes, blankets and mats etc., this equipment is used for playing house, cooking, hanging out the laundry on the "balcony" (= upper section), going down in the cellar (= an area dug out by the children under the playhouse. If it is not isolated and loose material suggested above not available, this equipment is **not** used for this kind of play.

Large combination equipment

Large combination equipment with wide slide, room formations on two levels, slanting roof, rope, rope ladder and net was used 115 minutes of 1480, or 7.85% of the time at two playgrounds. At a third no comparative time could be calculated since the whole playground was not under observation.

This equipment was used primarily for various exercise play, with the wide slide predominating and the alternative ways of getting up on the equipment and moving around it having most appeal. The smaller children play mostly peek-a-boo, and they require help and support if they are to climb up and slide down the slide. Joint games are common and children of different ages play together; children from three up to 10 or 12. Quiet pretend-games are rare since the equipment encourages play that is a bit too rough for such games. Rule-games such as how to slide, tag and no-touching-the-ground were played occasionally. This equipment appeals most to late-pre-school age and younger school children.

Large composite climbing equipment with slide, hammock, beams at various floor levels and with small roof has been used in varying degrees depending on how complete the composite equipment was and on which model was under observation. The equipment at Orminge was used 440 of 1660 minutes, which was 26.45% of the time (This figure is somewhat over-generous, see section on Orminge's playground.) The high frame with tower, rope and net at Tingvalla was used 95 of 1290 minutes, or 7.5% of the time.

There is no doubt that these climbing frames have a relatively high use frequency if they are placed where children have **few** other opportunities to climb. The fact that these climbing frames appeal to older children, who are badly catered for on our playgrounds, contributres to this high frequency of use. The big frames cannot be used by children under five without the aid of an adult. As regards the equipment at Orminge, both the wide slide and the hammock are too difficult to be mastered by the smaller children. The actual climbing frame itself has been shown to be too difficult for three- and four-year-olds to climb. From about the age of five the big climbing frames present a suitable challenge. Children of that age are able to climb up and jump in the jumping-mat and go up and down the slide, which they do with some intensity and in a variety of ways. Children from seven years and up use the whole of the composite equipment for playing tag and other games, and also pretend the equipment is a pirate ship. The version with tower and net is used too by children from five to 10 years old. Because it is high and there are only beams to walk on, it is difficult to go around it. A supplement section with a complete floor would make this frame more accessible to smaller children.

It is very important that high climbing frames are placed on soft ground or base to minimize falling injuries. Bits of tarpaulin, blankets, mats, pieces of masonite enhance their use.

"The knot" is a playground equipment system that can be structured differently from one place to another; it was used approximately 25% of the time (this figure is slightly high, see Sandvik description). **Three different** types of combination equipment are included in this figure within the same play area. The only alternative equipment available were swings and a sandpit.

"The knot" is suitable for children of varying age depending on which components are used. One of the obvious advantages to "the knot" is that its construction, unlike many other types of equipment, does not exclude the smallest children. The room-creating elements, the low creep-in, through which only the smaller children can enter, and steps that are well-designed for the smaller children, the low half-meter platforms, the varying slope angle of the slides and the double railings on the suspension bridge are all examples that show that the needs of smaller children have been taken into consideration in the designing of this equipment. The equipment was used mostly by children of three and four year old. They manage their way around the plateaus and suspension bridges with some excitement, and the conquest of their own fears. Usually they decide on rules as to how they may go around the equipment: three steps over the suspension bridge, count the planks, only walk on blue planks etc. Children over five have used their fantasy when playing on the quipment. Usually the equipment is likened to a ship or dock, and pretending they are blowing up bridges or setting the whole house on fire has also occurred. At the playground where "the knot" was supplemented with loose heavy benches and bits of planks, children of five and up chose to play on this equipment most. The loose supplementary material was used to experiment with; the children built a plank to balance on and used a leaning bench as a slide. Children over seven used the equipment only sporadically and then only the variants of "the knot" where they could move around it in different ways and play tag. Since there were few children over the age of seven in the areas where we observed "the knot", it is difficult to state how the equipment suited them.

"PAPRIKA"

"BJÖRN"

Games

Table-tennis tables were used 55 minutes of 8225, or 0.64% of the time.

Some of the possible reasons for the low frequency of use were the lack of proper wind screens, few older children at the playgrounds, and that during the period of our observatrions Bjorn Borg's success had made tennis much more popular than ping-pong. Our impression was that ping-pong tables are used much more frequently indoors. An arrangement we found in a number of parks and neighbourhood playgrounds.

Static representational equipment:

Animals

Animals anchored to the ground, a wooden pig, for instance, was used 1 minute of 1200, or 0.08% of the time. A horse and wagon was used 0 minutes of 626.

Wooden pigs placed together with a group of rocking-horses were used largely by adults to sit on. On one occasion a boy of about two years old tried to rock on one but went away disappointed.

The horse and wagon was also used occasionally to sit on and, according to the park personnel, sporadically for cowboy games, or children pretended they were going on a trip, but mostly it remained empty.

Animals that could be rolled around, such as the wooden snail, were used 14 of 1280 minutes, or 1.09% of the time.

It is mostly younger children who climb up to ride on "the horse". Usually the children rolled the snail about and regarded it as a horse or a cannon. Because the snail is included in a group consisting of a hut and a train, the "horse" has a given role in play at this playground. One child's comment tells us something of the dangers of fixed representational equipment: "It's not a horse. It's a bang-bang."

Vehicles

Boats were used 67 minutes of 1190, or 5.63% of the time.

Those boats studied were, on the whole, more or less like boats. One variant which consisted only of a mast and two rounded sections of concrete was not used for play. On the other hand, boats with railings, mast etc. were used for balancing and climbing and for imaginative games related to boating, diving and swimming. It is obvious that children's experience of boats and the sea and the possible inspirational influence of adults, play an important role in the course such play takes. As we noted earlier, equipment which is not representationally **fixed** can easily be made to represent a boat if the children so wish.

Play sculptures

Play sculptures of plastic, Pepper and Bear, were used 30 minutes of 510, or 5.9% of the time.

It is primarily the age group from three to seven that play with the plastic sculptures. The smaller children find it difficult to climb up on them and play instead in the sand under the figures. It is mainly the possibility of using the Peppers as a slide that appeals to children over three. The most attractive features appear to be the different ways of getting up on the sculpture and the fact that the slide ends in a tunnel. The plastic sculptures are often likened to boats. Imaginative play such as diving and swimming, and games such as police and thief occur among five- and six-year-olds. The undefined form seems to appeal to the children's fantasy.

Play sculpture of metal, a dragon that can spurt water, was used 85 minutes of 910, or 9.25% of the time.

Since the dragon was put up during the observation time, the figure can only represent a high **newness** value. Briefly, we can only say that the

dragon was a well-needed break in all the mass-produced equipment for children, and another positive aspect is that the sculpture was designed as a symbol for the area, called **Drakenberg** (Mount Dragon). Play is encouraged mostly by the spurting of water and climbing and riding the dragon. The slide on the dragon's trail is, on the other hand, dangerous.

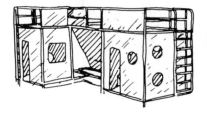

Tree trunks

Tree trunks were used 18 of 2170 minutes, or 0.8% of the time.

Tree trunks were used mostly by adults to sit down, for want of anything better. The tree trunks appealed primarily to the smaller children. They creep, climb or ride on them. A hollow tree trunk encourages peek-a-boo games and the children enjoy crawling inside them to experience the contrast between light and darkness. If the surface of the tree trunk is uneven so that water may collect in places, the children find this interesting. Older children have sometimes played horse or climbed and rocked in the limbs, or lay their cheeks against it to feel the soft, smooth wood.

Room-creating equipment:

Huts

Small huts with roofs were used 50 minutes of 3550, or 1.37% of the time.

It is primarily the smallest children who go in and out of huts, pour sand on the floor (where there is one) and sweep it away again. In certain playgrounds huts act as supplements to combination equipment or representational equipment. A hut may act as a place to which one "goes home" or "visits". Mostly the huts have been placed too much in the open for any imaginative play to develop. Nor have the children had access to pieces of cloth and blankets to add to them. A complement of sand is simply not enough.

Small huts without roof were used 11 minutes of 2305, or 0.47% of the time.

At the five different playgrounds where we observed such huts they were hardly used at all. When children approached them they merely climbed in and out again. Thus the huts functioned as low climbing frames. Since the children lacked cloth, mats, pieces of masonite etc. with which to build roofs, room-creating did not interest them at all. It would appear that a roof is of great importance if children are to feel enclosed.

Screens

Commercial screens were used 11 minutes of 1300, or 0.85% of the time.

Play screens are an obvious example of how meaningless fixed equipment becomes when it is placed in areas where the children have no access to berries, pine cones, leaves, branches, or where they cannot safely store such "treasures" as a cup without a handle, an empty snuff box, a discarded teapot. The play screens were used once or twice to climb on, and on **one** occasion as a store. This was when children had decided to take discarded bottles and beer cans from refuse baskets. Play that was soon stopped by adults.

Towers

Lookout towers were used 50 minutes of 3610, or 1.4% of the time.

Towers were used by children from about three years and up. The smaller children climb them and were primarily aiming at daring and overcoming their fear of height. The older children who could easily climb them and no longer feared height usually played pretend-games such as war, or sat in the seclusion of the towers together and talked. A place to climb up, to feel big, so big that no adult can reach them, and someplace to withdraw to, to hide, to be alone, is needed at every children's playground. The potential for choosing between seclusion and togetherness is best achieved by taking advantage of and enhancing the natural variations in vagetation and landscape. In those cases where the natural environment does not allow for the possibility of climbing a few meters up, a tower, for instance, may be a good thing.

Play towers of plastic, with two levels and lookout porthole were used 36 minutes of 1295, or 2.8% of the time.

This tower was used sporadically by children aged three to seven. Mainly children climbed for brief periods or played in the sand below. On a few occasions fantasy games were played.

Playhouses

Blue playhouse in two levels, separate rooms and a narrow ladder on the outside. The playhouse was used 195 minutes of 1800, or 10.7% of the time.

The playhouse has been shown to adapt well to many types of play and games, and appeals to children from one and two up to 10 to 12 years of age. Because the bars of the ladder are placed close together and it does not lean at a treacherous angle, it is suitable even for smaller children. The separate rooms, lookout holes that give a sense of light and dark contrasts appeal to the smallest children's need for peek-a-boo games and to move about in a secure way at heights. The playhouse encourages play together; the children chase each other in the playhouse and on the roof. They jump on the roof together, shout and laugh. Usually adults are recruited into games of peek-a-boo and tag. The playhouse has **not** functioned especially well for pretend-games. Only the **onset** of such play has occurred. This type of play would probably increase if the playhouse contained some storage space where the children could hide their "treasures", such as saucers and bits of cloth etc. Thus this equipment has had a lower frequency of use among those age groups where pretend-games are most common: 4-7. On the other hand, older children have used it more, since a playhouse encourages them to chase each other and indulge in rule-games such as tag.

Playhouse, storage module, simple shed with walls and flat roof was used 24 of 694 minutes, or 3.45% of the time.

The storage module has been shown to have many functions and offers opportunities both for climbing and pretend-games. One clear advantage with this equipment is that its simple design does not "lock" the children as to **how** they use it, whether for climbing, or what it is to represent in their play. The smaller children have used the area under the roof mostly. They play baker and family. From about the age of five the children are able to climb up on the module's roof. The broad cracks or spaces between the planks are an advantage in that the children can fasten cardboard in them to make shelves. This has been done among the older children in their more advanced role-games. Another advantage to the module playhouse is that it can "follow" children, as it were, through the years, so that when the smaller children grow older within a neighbourhood, the module can then function as a bicycle rack or workshop.

Playhouses

Playhouses of traditional type were used 50 minutes of 1530, or 3.3% of the time.

The low frequency of use was caused largely by the fact that the playhouses were not available to children during the whole period of observation. The figure is for supervised playgrounds where, to the extent the playhouses were open, the children had access to old clothes to "dress up in", dolls, doll beds, curtains, masonite sheets etc. A playhouse at an unsupervised playground was used 1.2% of the time. This playhouse was placed beside a large climbing frame, which meant that quiet, lasting play never really began. Playhouses have been shown to function well for children from one to 10 years old, although children from five to 10 played there most. The playhouse encourages to a high degree pretend- and role-games that are so important for children's development. Usually children of different ages play together and boys and girls both join in role-games, even though some play took place with sex-separate roles. The most common type of play concerned family games. The smaller children act as "children", they dress up, go visiting, go to work, shop: that is to say, recover leaves, gather sticks, cook, put the children to bed, sleep, change diapers, read fairy tales, clean up, put up curtains etc. The games have had elements of inventivness and experimental activity. The children have built a sofa of blocks, or tested ways of climbing up on the roof with the help of a chair.

If the playhouse is to function properly it is necessary to place it in a quiet area and preferably within a group of other playhouses or huts. Toys such as dolls and loose materials such as furnishings of bits of cloth and masonite enhance the games. Details like floors (to sweep), doors, window openings etc. have been shown to have some importance for how children play.

It is common that children use the playhouse to climb on, especially during the colder season of the year. Therefore the houses should be placed on soft ground and in such a way that they do not encourage jumping from one roof to another.

Rain and wind cover

The rain-cover house **with** climbing net was used 35 minutes of 670, or 5.4% of the time.
Rain-cover house **without** climbing net was used 14 of 810 minutes, or 1.7% of the time.

The rain house appeals primarily to exercise activity and social togetherness among children from five years and up. The smaller children climb on the benches and net, play peek-a-boo, or look on as the older children climb up the "shelves" of the house or on its roof. There are alternative ways of climbing up for the older children. The easiest way is up the net, but children have even succeeded in finding ways up the beams. By making the climbing more difficult a challenge is introduced that is an important element in play. Rain houses have been used in conjunction with other equipment at playgrounds. The children can have played tag among the various pieces of equipment or have "home" in each his own playhouse. The play has often been rather wild and physically lively. This goes for both the pretend-games and rule-games that were played.

Since the house is used for climbing, it should be placed on a soft base. One should note that removal of the net does not stop the children from climbing up on it. A rain house contributes to **adults** remaining at the playground, despite light rain now and then. In consideration of how valuable this is to the children, and the value of rain and the subsequent pools of water in children's play, the rain house can be a definite advantage at unsupervised playgrounds.* The rain and wind-covers we have studied at excessively windy playgrounds were **not** used by children or adults.

*The rain house cannot replace thorough planning in the creation of a good and suitable environment.

Constructive materials:

Building sets

Building boxes were used 320 minutes of 3930, or 8.15% of the time. The frequency of use varied, so that at two playgrounds it was 4-5%, 8.3% in one, and a little more than 13% in two park playgrounds. It should be noted that building boxes were not always unlocked and accessible to the children.

The building boxes were used by children from one to 13, but primarily by children from three to 10. There is a challenge for the smallest children just in lugging the heavy blocks about and lifting them in and out of the box and perhaps piling them up. By using the loose ladder the small child can even climb into the box, which provides a crowded and interesting room-creation. The larger children too use the box as a place to withdraw to, to eat an apple or to talk to a friend. From about the age of three the box is also used in pretend-games. The box is often likened to a "boat" or a "house". Five- and six-year-olds, who are the ones who use the building box most and stay with it longest, often use all the material to build large constructions together. Both pretend-games and problem-solving are common: the children may try to get a plank to balance evenly or test various ways of building. In the 7-10 age group the pretend-games begin to acquire more and more realistic elements and the children's roles in the play gain further nuances, so that the persons involved complement each other rather than merely copy one another. Examples of the games played are: store, ships and warfare with cannon, defending "gold bars" with a machine-gun, building a home with beds, blankets, fireplace, kitchen sink and TV etc. In one or two cases children over 10 used the building blocks. Children of this age prefer hammers, nails and boards. In lthe larger park playgrounds, two building boxes can be advantageously placed next to each other.

Sand boxes

Sand boxes or pits were studied at 26 playgrounds and were used on the average 18.7% of the time. Frequency of use varied between approx. 10% and up to 50%, due partly to what other alternatives were available to the children. The frequency of use is generally higher at unsupervised playgrounds: 23.1%, while the average at supervised playgrounds was 17.0%.

Anyone wishing to know how much children play in sand should be warned that the above figures are, on the whole, a low estimate. This is partly because we have not studied those sections of supervised playgrounds described as playpens, and partly because children play to a **great extent** in sand under the playground equipment. Sand is one of the few materials at playgrounds that provides children with an opportunity to express, through their own imagination and creativity, their experience of the reality around them. Playing in sand appeals to children from 0 years up to 10 or 12. The smallest children enjoy just messing in it, feeling it and tasting it and filling and emptying their pails. When the small child seeks to grasp the world around him and tests cause and effect, the best materials for these experiments are those that change, such as sand, snow, water, clay, blocks, which enable the child to see the effects of his/her actions. Sand encourages very **small** children to pretend. They drive their cars in it, bake cakes and cookies. As the child grows older and his abilities increase, the range of his play in sand expands. Children build roads, hills, dig pits through to China, sprinkle "sugar" using dry sand and note the tire tracks of cars in wet sand. Equipment such as mechanical shovels, wheelbarrows and rakes are used in their play, and the children pretend they are "working", mixing asphalt or digging. Sometimes they "dig for gold" and often they enjoy burying themselves or a friend wholly in sand. Playing together is a common activity in sand boxes, even though children will also play alone, especially when they are small. From about the age of five years and up children will often construct whole landscapes and communities, the source of which is often their play with cars. These games often progress during intense discussions about "how it is" and frequently lead to conflicts of the type "you can't drive on my road", which, when the children solve them, give some insight into the advantages in sharing, of playing together and helping each other. The rule-games that occurred were broad-jump and racing around the sand box. Since children of different ages use the sand differently, it is advantageous to have more than one sand box available within a particular area, and not merely one near the door for the smallest children, but also another one in a more secluded place for the bigger children. The sand box should have many corners so as to allow a number of children to find a place of their own, to play by themselves or together in small groups. To achieve this the sand box may be placed with advantage beside an outcrop, allowing the edge of the sand box to follow the existing variations in the surface of the ground. It is primarily the older children who make use of the free area of sand. They wrestle in the sand or build big forts or community systems. Therefore it is very important that the sand boxes are not blocked by fixed playground equipment. Indeed this is a safety requirement, since children playing on the equipment may fall on those playing in the sand. Further conditions in assuring properly functioning sand play are the availability of water and some protection against the sun, wind and rain. The depth of the sand should be 80 cm. According to **Children's Outdoor Milieu** (Barns utemiljo - SOU 1970:1) the depth of sand for smaller children should be at least half-a-meter, and at least **one-meter** for bigger children.